# A TABLE ALPHABETICALL
## OF HARD USUAL ENGLISH WORDS

# *A Table Alphabeticall*

*of Hard Usual English Words*
(1604)

**The First English Dictionary**

BY

ROBERT CAWDREY

A FACSIMILE REPRODUCTION
WITH AN INTRODUCTION
BY

ROBERT A. PETERS

SCHOLARS' FACSIMILES & REPRINTS
DELMAR, NEW YORK, 1976

First reprinted by
Scholars' Facsimiles & Reprints
in 1966
Second printing 1976

Reproduced from a copy in
and with the permission of
The Bodleian Library
University of Oxford

Printed in the United States of America

**Library of Congress Cataloging Data**
Cawdry, Robert.
A table alphabeticall
of hard usual English words (1604).
Original t.p. reads: A table alphabeticall,
conteyning and teaching the true writing,
and understanding of hard usuall English wordes,
borrowed from the Hebrew,
Greeke, Latine, or French. &c. . . .
London, Printed by I.R.
for Edmund Weaver, 1604.
1. English language—Dictionaries—
Early Works to 1700.
I. Title.
PE1620.C3 1604a    423    66-12119
ISBN  0-8201-1007-8

# INTRODUCTION

Robert Cawdrey's *A Table Alphabeticall* (1604), important as the first edition of the first English dictionary, constitutes a lexicographic milestone. More than that, it is important as a mirror of late-Elizabethan attitudes toward life and reality as reflected in the definitions of the approximately 2,500 entries in the dictionary. The definition of *meteors* as 'elementarie bodies, or moyst things, ingendered of vapours in the ayre aboue' clearly is indicative of a bygone age. So too is the definition of *matron* as 'an auncient, sober, and a discreete woman,' of *driblets* as 'small debts,' of *concubine* as a 'harlot, or light huswife,' and of *theology* as 'diuinitie, the science of liuing blessedly for euer.'

The entries from *Abandon* to *Zodiack* in the dictionary also provide a kaleidoscope of varying hues and interest. The entries *abricot* 'kind of fruit' and *nevewe* 'a sonne or daughters sonne' indicate to the historical linguist the use in 1600 of a voiced stop and fricative, respectively, in *apricot* and *nephew*. The student of the history of punctuation will note the absence of the apostrophe in the possessive singular 'daughters sonne' above. The misprints *virinitie* for *vicinitie* and *grogresse* for *progresse* will remind the modern editor of the error that flesh is heir to. For the student of etymology, the derivational suffix-*ick(e)* in *eth-*

*nick* 'an heathen or gentile' and *neotericke* 'one of late time' will call to mind modern *sputnik* and *beatnik*. The entry *overplus* 'more than needeth' will suggest to the sensitive reader its similarity to modern governmentese and Orwell's Newspeak. Many additional examples of interest could be cited, but to do so surely would lessen the reader's joy of self-discovery in examining the *Table*.

The dictionary by Cawdrey was not his first editorial product. According to Pollard and Redgrave's *A Short-Title Catalogue*, Cawdrey also is credited with two earlier works: 1. *A short and fruitefull treatise of the profit of catechising* (1580, augmented edition 1604), and 2. *A treasurie or store-house of similes* (1600, another issue in 1609).

Unfortunately, little is known about Cawdrey's life. In the Dedicatorie to the *Table*, Cawdrey tells us that at one time he taught "the Grammer Schoole at Okeham in the County of Rutland" in east central England. He adds that the *Table* "long ago for the most part, was gathered by me, but lately augmented by my sonne Thomas, who now is Schoolemaister in London." As such Thomas should be given partial if not equal credit as co-author of the *Table*. In addition, the *Dictionary of National Biography* lists a younger son, Daniel Cawdrey (1588-1664).

By his own account Cawdrey had a connection of sorts with the Harington family of Rutlandshire, at least an indebtedness for patronage. In

INTRODUCTION vii

the Epistle, dated 27 June 1604, prefatory to the *Table,* Cawdrey dedicated his work to the "naturall sisters" Lady Hastings, Lady Dudley, Lady Mountague, Lady Wingfield, and Lady Leigh. He also mentions Lady Lucie Harington, "your Honours and Worships mother," and Sir James Harington, "Knight, your Ladiships brother, ... my scholler, (and now my singuler benefactor) when I taught the Grammer Schoole at Okeham."

As is known, the Harington Family is not without literary associations. James, the younger brother of Sir John Harington (d. 1613), first Baron Harington (21 July 1603) of Exton Hall, Rutland, was the cousin of Sir John Harington (1561-1612), metrical translator of Ariosto's *Orlando Furioso.* James also was the grandfather of James Harington (or Harrington), author of the political romance *The Commonwealth of Oceana* (1656). The mother, Lady Lucie, was the sister of Sir Henry Sidney, father of Sir Philip Sidney the poet.

Perhaps Cawdrey's unique contribution to the field of English lexicography can best be appreciated when it is contrasted with the centuries-long tradition of vocabulary study in England that preceded the publication of the *Table.* That tradition, as also in the case of grammar, dates back to the Anglo-Saxon period and the study of Latin. As various studies inform, Latin was studied in the monastic schools in Anglo-Saxon England, not the vernacular we call English, which evolved from the Germanic dialects carried to Britain by

## INTRODUCTION

invaders from the northwestern fringe of Europe beginning in the fifth century A.D. Latin, not English, was studied because it was the international written and spoken medium of medieval Europe; it was the written form in which religious materials were preserved; and it was the spoken form in which the church conducted mass.

So it was that then, as now, schoolboys studying Latin texts encountered words and phrases that caused them difficulty or relative difficulty in translation. So it was then, also, as now, that students inserted simpler Latin or English synonyms for the "hard" terms in their texts as aids in study and translation. Subsequently, such interlinear and marginal glosses of hard terms, largely Scriptural in nature, were collected and compacted into handy reference lists. Thus, vocabulary study in England originated with the practice of compiling pedagogical lists of Latin word demons and their glosses as aids in the study of Latin.

The earliest of such extant Old English word lists is *The Corpus Glossary*, which is preserved in an eighth- or ninth-century manuscript.[1] Similar to the alphabetical list of Latin-Latin and Latin-Old English words in *Corpus* are the *Leiden, Epinal,* and *Erfurt Glossaries* of the same period.[2] A later Latin-Old English list (10th cent.) is that of Aelfric, abbot and scholar.[3] Other Latin-Old

---

[1] See W. M. Lindsay, *The Corpus Glossary, Publications of the Philological Society,* VIII (Oxford, 1921).

[2] See Henry Sweet, *The Oldest English Texts, EETS,* 83 (1885).

[3] See J. Zupitza, *Aelfrics Grammatik und Glossar* (Berlin, 1880).

# INTRODUCTION ix

English glossaries also survive from the Old English period, but they are relatively minor.[4]

The pedagogical practice of collecting study lists of difficult terms continued throughout the Middle English period in connection with the study of Latin and later also of French. One such Middle English vocabulary list is Alexander Neckham's Latin-French-English *De nominibus utensilium* (c. 1200).[5] Other representatives of the period are the English-Latin *Promptorium parvulorum sive clericorum* 'a storeroom for young scholars' (c. 1440) and its Latin-English companion the [*H*]*Ortus vocabulorum*, printed in 1499 and 1500 respectively.[6] A later compilation is the English-Latin *Catholicon Anglicum* (c. 1483).[7]

In the early portion of the Early Modern English period, the tradition of compiling bilingual and multilingual vocabulary lists received fresh impetus following the introduction of printing to England by William Caxton. Such compendia, and schoolbooks, include the Latin-English *Vocabula* (1496) and *Vulgaria* (1508) of John Stanbridge, the Latin-English *Dictionary of Syr Thomas Eliot* (1538), Richard Huloet's *Abcedar-*

[4] See Thomas Wright and Richard P. Wülcker, *Anglo-Saxon and Old English Vocabularies* (London, 1884). 2 vols.
[5] See Thomas Wright, *A Volume of Vocabularies* (London, 1857).
[6] See A. L. Mayhew, *EETSES*, CII (1908).
[7] See S. J. Herrtage and H. B. Wheatley, *EETS*, 75 (1881).

INTRODUCTION

*ium Anglo-Latinum* (1552), John Withal's English-Latin *A shorte dictionarie for younge begynners* (1553), Thomas Cooper's *Thesaurus Linguae Romanae & Britannicae* (1565), John Baret's English-Latin-French-Greek *Alvearie or Quadruple Dictionary* (1573), Thomas Thomas' *Dictionarium Linguae Latinae et Anglicanae* (1587), and John Rider's English-Latin *Bibliotheca scholastica* (1589), to mention some examples.[8]

In the sixteenth century several factors contributed to the growing emergence into respectability of the English vernacular and ultimately an interest in the vocabulary of English. One such factor was the scholarly controversy about the vagaries of English spelling, which dispute was eventually resolved by printers and "correctors" through the development of a more or less standard or fixed system of English spelling.[9] A second factor was the scholarly argument concerning the legitimacy of English as a vehicle of composition; this issue eventually subsided in the wake of printed translations in English of classical and foreign language materials, including the Bible. A third factor was the introduction, first, into pettie or elementary schools and, later, into grammar or secondary schools of English as a subject of study, perhaps in part as a result of

[8] See DeWitt T. Starnes, *Renaissance Dictionaries English-Latin and Latin-English* (Austin, 1954).
[9] For a discussion of the various controversies about English in the EModE period, see Richard F. Jones, *The Triumph of the English Language* (Stanford, 1953).

criticism that knowledge of Latin was of little practical benefit in the everyday world of business and life. A fourth factor was the publication of various English-modern language dictionaries and manuals (grammar plus vocabulary) stemming from interest in such languages as French, Spanish, and Italian, stimulated in part by expanding commercial trade.[10] A fifth factor was the scholarly debate that centered about the introduction by English writers of numerous loanwords from the Continent and the resurrection of archaisms from earlier periods of English. Difficulties that readers encountered with such pedantic or inkhorn terms contributed directly to the need for vocabulary lists of hard English words, especially those of foreign origin.

One work of that genre was Edmund Coote's *The English Schoole-Master* (1596). Although Coote's work contains an Early Modern English

[10]They include John Palsgrave's French-English *Lesclarcissement de la langue francoyse* (1530), William Salesbury's *A Dictionary in Englyshe and Welshe* (1547), William Thomas' *Principal rules of the Italian grammer, with a dictionarie* (1550) John Veron's Latin-French-English *Dictionariolum puerorum tribus linguis* (1552), Claudius Hollyband's English-French *The French Schoole-Maister* (1573), John Florio's English-Italian *Florio His firste Fruites* (1578), William Stepney's English-Spanish *The Spanish Schoolemaster* (1591), and Hollyband's *A Dictionarie French and English* (1593). See also H. S. Bennett, *English Books and Readers 1475 to 1557* (Cambridge, 1952), pp 85-97; E. J. Dobson, *English Pronunciation* 1500-1700 (Oxford, 1957) II, 1011-12.

vocabulary list of about 1,500 hard words, his publication is essentially an eclectic primer of catechism, prayers, and grammar, plus vocabulary. Thus, Coote's volume cannot actually be regarded as a true dictionary, although in point of time Coote's word list may be recognized as the immediate precursor to the first English dictionary, namely Cawdrey's *Table Alphabeticall*.

As we come full circle to the *Table* it is necessary to avow Cawdrey's debt—unacknowledged by himself—for material taken from Coote's vocabulary list and from Thomas' Latin-English dictionary. Those details have been fully treated elsewhere by Professors DeWitt T. Starnes and Gertrude E. Noyes,[11] and, as such, they need not be entered into here.

However, it should be pointed out that Cawdrey's generous borrowing from several sources was not altogether out of keeping with the tradition of such practice in the Middle English and Early Modern English periods, when originality of materials and treatment was not a necessary prerequisite for authorship. Nor, it can be said, is that practice dead today. At any rate, Cawdrey's plagiarism, if that is the correct term, should not diminish or subtract from his real contribution of producing in England the first volume devoted exclusively to an alphabetical

[11] *The English Dictionary from Cawdrey to Johnson* 1604-1755 (Chapel Hill, 1946), pp 13-18. See also Noyes, "The First English Dictionary, Cawdrey's *Table Alphabeticall, MLN*, LVIII (1943), 600-5.

# INTRODUCTION xiii

listing of English words explained by other English words, instead of words from some other language, like Latin. In comparison to Coote, Cawdrey also must be credited with providing more amplified definitions and synonyms in his selective vocabulary list of contemporary "hard" words.

As the title page of the *Table* announces, Cawdrey's work was intended for an audience other than schoolboys but one nevertheless relatively untutored. Cawdrey's preface also reveals his interest in the vocabulary controversy of his day concerning "ynckhorne termes."[12] He admonishes those that counterfeit the King's English with foreign terms "that they forget altogether their mothers language, so that if some of their mothers were aliue, they were not able to tell, or vnderstand what they say." Instead, in the Statement to the Reader, Cawdrey pedagogically advises his audience to use the "plainest & best kind of speech" and to employ primarily "such words as wee vse."

That Cawdrey's work found a popular reception is evidenced by the fact that the *Table* had three later editions: the second (date unknown), the third (1613), and the fourth (1617). Apart from a slightly expanded word list, the later editions were without significant changes in text from the first edition.[13]

[12]"English Dictionaries of the Seventeenth Century," *University of Texas Studies in English*, XVII (July, 1937), 20-24.
[13]Starnes and Noyes, *English Dictionary*, p. 19.

## INTRODUCTION

Thus the first English dictionary was given birth in 1604 in Cawdrey's *Table Alphabeticall.* The format and legacy of that work persist to the present day, augmented only by amplification—pronunciation, accentuation, etymologies. Such supplementary features appeared 123 years after Cawdrey's work in the first modern dictionary, the second edition of Nathaniel Bailey's *Universal Etymological Dictionary of the English Language* (1727). Accordingly, we may posit a three-stage development in the evolution of the English dictionary: the bilingual and the later multilingual stage as initiated perhaps by *The Corpus Glossary,* the English hard-words stage as initiated by Cawdrey's *Table,* and the modern stage as initiated by Bailey's *Universal Etymological Dictionary.*

I wish to express my appreciation to the Keeper of Printed Books at the Bodleian Library for kind permission to reprint this only known surviving copy from holdings in that excellent library.

R. A. PETERS

*Western Washington State College*
*Bellingham, Washington*

# A
# Table Alphabeticall, con-
teyning and teaching the true vvriting, and vnderstanding of hard vsuall English wordes, borrowed from the Hebrew, Greeke, Latine, or French. &c.

With the interpretation thereof by *plaine English words, gathered for the benefit & helpe of Ladies, Gentlewomen, or any other vnskilfull persons.*

Whereby they may the more easilie and better vnderstand many hard English wordes, vvhich they shall heare or read in Scriptures, Sermons, or elswhere, and also be made able to vse the same aptly themselues.

*Legere, et non intelligere, neglegere est.*
As good not read, as not to vnderstand.

AT LONDON,
Printed by I. R. for Edmund Weauer, & are to be sold at his shop at the great North doore of Paules Church.
1604.

# To the right honourable,

Worshipfull, vertuous, & godlie Ladies, the Lady Hastings, the Lady Dudley, the Lady Mountague, the Ladie Wingfield, and the Lady Leigh, his Christian friends, R. C. wisheth great prosperitie in this life, with increase of grace, and peace from GOD our Father, through Iesus Christ our Lord and onely Sauiour.

BY this Table (right Honourable & Worshipfull) strangers that blame our tongue of difficultie, and vncertaintie may heereby plainly see, & better vnderstand those things, which they haue thought hard. Heerby also the true Orthography, that is, the true writing of many hard English words, borrowed from the Greeke, Latine & French, and how to know one from the other, with the interpretation thereof by plaine English words, may be learned and knowne. And children heereby may be prepared for the vnderstanding of a great number of Latine words: which also will bring much delight & iudgement to others, by the vse of this little worke. Which worke, long ago for the most part, was gathered by me, but lately augmented by my sonne Thomas, who now is Schoolemaister in London.

## The Epistle.

Now when I had called to mind (right honorable and Worshipfull) the great kindnesse, and bountifulnes, which I found in that vertuous & godly Lady, Lucie Harington, your Honours and Worships mother, and my especiall friend in the Lord. When, and at such time as the right Worshipfull Sir Iames Harington Knight, your Ladiships brother was my scholler, (and now my singuler benefactor) when I taught the Grammer schoole at Okeham in the County of Rutland: In consideration whereof, and also for that I acknowledge my selfe much beholding and indebted to the most of you, since this time, (beeing all naturall sisters) I am bold to make you all ioyntly patrons heereof, and vnder your names to publish this simple worke. And thus praying, that God of his vnspeakeable mercies, will blesse both your Honors and Worships, I doe with all good wishes to you all, with all yours, as to mine owne soule, humbly take my leaue. Couentry this xxvij. of Iune. 1604.

Your Honors and Worships, euer ready in Christ Iesus to be commaunded, *Robert Cawdrey.*

## To the Reader.

Such as by their place and calling, (but especially Preachers) as haue occasion to speak publiquely before the ignorant people, are to bee admonished, that they neuer affect any strange ynckhorne termes, but labour to speake so as is commonly receiued, and so as the most ignorant may well vnderstand them: neyther seeking to be ouer fine or curious, nor yet liuing ouer carelesse, vsing their speech, as most men doe, & ordering their wits, as the fewest haue done. Some men seek so far for outlandish English, that they forget altogether their mothers language, so that if some of their mothers were aliue, they were not able to tell, or vnderstand what they say, and yet these fine English Clearks, will say they speak in their mother tongue; but one might well charge them, for counterfeyting the Kings English. Also, some far iournied gentlemē, at their returne home, like as they loue to go in forraine apparrell, so they will pouder their talke with ouer-sea language. He that commeth lately out of France, will talk French English, and neuer blush at the matter.

## To the Reader.

matter. Another chops in with English Italianated, and applyeth the Italian phrase to our English speaking, the which is, as if an Orator, that professeth to vtter his minde in plaine Latine, would needs speake Poetrie, & far fetched colours of strange antiquitie. Doth any wise man think, that wit resteth in strange words, or els stãdeth it not in wholsome matter, and apt declaring of a mans mind? Do we not speak, because we would haue other to vnderstand vs? or is not the tongue giuen for this end, that one might know what another meaneth? Therefore, either wee must make a difference of English, & say, some is learned English, & othersome is rude English, or the one is Court talke, the other is Country-speech, or els we must of necesitie banish all affected Rhetorique, and vse altogether one manner of language. Those therefore that will auoyde this follie, and acquaint themselues with the plainest & best kind of speech, must seeke frõ time to time such words as are cõmonlie receiued, and such as properly may expresse in plaine manner, the whole conceit of their mind. And looke what words wee best vnderstand, and know what they meane, the
same

## To the Reader.

same should soonest be spoken, and first applied, to the vtterance of our purpose. Therfore for this end, foure things would chiefly be obserued in the choise of wordes. First, that such words as wee vse, should be proper vnto the tongue wherein we speake. Againe, that they be plaine for all men to perceiue. Thirdly, that they be apt and meete, most properly to set out the matter. Fourthlie, that words translated, from one signification to another, (called of the Grecians *Tropes*,) be vsed to beautifie the sentence, as precious stones are set in a ring, to cōmend the gold. Now such are thought apt words, that properly agree vnto that thing, which they signifie, and plainly expresse the nature of the same. Therefore, they that haue regard of their estimation and credite, do warily speake, & with choise, vtter words most apt for their purpose. In waightie causes, graue wordes are thought most needfull, that the greatnes of the matter, may the rather appeare, in the vehemencie of theyr talke. So likewise of other, like order must be taken. Albeit some, not onely doe not obserue this kind of aptnesse, but also they fall into much fondnes, by vsing words out of

## To the Reader.

of place, and applying them to diuers matters, without all discretion.

If thou be desirous (gentle Reader) rightly and readily to vnderstand, and to profit by this Table, and such like, then thou must learne the Alphabet, to wit, the order of the Letters as they stand, perfectly without booke, and where euery Letter standeth: as (b) neere the beginning, (n) about the middest, and (t) toward the end. Nowe if the word, which thou art desirous to finde, begin with (a) then looke in the beginning of this Table, but if with (v) looke towards the end. Againe, if thy word beginne with (ca) looke in the beginning of the letter (c) but if with (cu) then looke toward the end of that letter. And so of all the rest. &c.

And further vnderstand, that whereas all such words as are deriued & drawne frō the Greek, are noted with these letter, (g). And the French are marked thus (§) but such words as are deriued from the latin, haue no marke at all.

# A Table Alphabeticall,

contayning and teaching the true writing, and vnderstanding of hard *vsuall English words. &c.*

(∴)

(k) standeth for a kind of.
(g. or gr.) standeth for Greeke.
The French words haue this (§) before them.

## A

§ Abandon, cast away, or yælde vp, to leaue, or forsake.
Abash, blush.
abba, father.
§ abbesse, abbatesse, Mistris of a Nunnerie, comforters of others.
§ abbettors, counsellors.
aberration, a going a stray, or wandering.
abbreuiat, } to shorten, or make
§ abbridge, } short.
§ abbut, to lie vnto, or border vpon, as one lands end meets with another.
abecedarie, the order of the Letters, or hee that vseth them.
aberration, a going astray, or wandering.
§ abet, to maintaine.

B.  § abdi-

An Alphabeticall table

abdicate, put away, refuse, or forsake.
abhorre, hate, despise, or disdaine.
abiect, base, cast away, in disdaine:
abiure, renounce, denie, forsweare:
abolish,    ⎱ make voyde, destroy, deface,
abolited,  ⎰ or out of vse.
§ abortiue, borne before the time.
abricot, (k) kind of fruit:
abrogate, take away, disanull, disallow,
abruptly, vnorderly, without a preface.
absolue, finish, or acquite:
absolute, perfect, or vpright.
absolution, forgiuenes, discharge:
abstract, drawne away frō another: a litte booke or volume gathered out of a greater.
absurd, foolish, irksome.
academie, an Vniuersitie, as Cambridge, or Oxford:
academicke, of the sect of wise and learned men.
accent, tune, the rising or falling of ye voice.
accept, to take liking of, or to entertaine willingly.
§ acceptāce, an agræing to some former act done before.
accesse, free cōming to, or a way to a place,
accesꝫ

## of hard English words.

accessarie, partaker in the same thing
§ accessorie, an accident extraordinary
accident, a chance, or happening.
accidentall, falling by chance, not by nature
accomodate, to make fit to, or conuenient to the purpose
§ accomplish, finish, or make an end of.
accommodating, lending
§ account, reckon.
§ accord, agreement between persons
accurate, curious, cunning, diligent.
§ accrew, grow, increase, goe.
§ acertaine, make sure, certifie.
acetositie, sharpnes, or sowernesse
§ acheeue, to make an end of
§ acquitall, discharge
acquisition, getting, purchasing
§ action, the forme of a suite
actiue, nimble, ready, quicke.
actuall, in act, or shewing it selfe in deed
acute, sharp, wittie, quick
adage, an old speech, or prouerbe,
adamantine, as hard as Diamont
addict, giuen to, appointed to
adhærent, cleauing to, or taking part with.
§ adiew, farewell
§ addresse, prepare, or direct.

An Alphabeticall table
adiacint, lying too, adioyning too
adiunct, an accidentall qualitie, or any propertie, that is not a substance.
§ adiourne, deferre, or put off till another
  time.
adiure, make to sweare, or to deny
administer, gouerne, serue, or rule, or doe
  seruice vnto
administrator, one that doth busines for an
  other
admire, maruell at, or be in loue with
admiration, wonderment, reioycing
§ admirall, chiefe by sea, worthy
admission, receiuing, or leaue to enter into
  a place, accept.
adopt, to take for his child, freely to choose
§ adore, worship, or reuerence,
adorne, beautifie, apparrell, prepare.
§ aduaunce, preferre, lift vp to honor:
aduent, the comming
aduerse, contrary, or backward
§ aduertise, giue knowledge, aduise, or counsell:
adulation, flatterie, or fauning
adulterate, to counterfeit, or corrupt:
aduocate, a spokesman, atturney, or man
  of law, plead.
§ aduowson,

## of hard English words.

§ aduousion, patronage, or power to present, or giue a liuing.
adustion, burning, or rosting.

Æ., see E.

affable, readie, and curteous in spéech, gracious in words.
§ affaires, busines
§ affect, to desire earnestly, or to mind
affected, disposed, inclined
affinitie, kinne by marriage
affirme, auouch, acertaine
§ affiance, trust
§ affianced, betrothed
§ affranchise, set at libertie.
agent, doer, a steward, or commissioner
aggrauate, make more grieuous, and more heauie:
agilitie, nimblenes, or quicknes
agglutinate, to ioyne together
agnition, knowledge, or acknowledging
agitate, driuen, stirred, tossed
agonie, (gr) heauie passion, anguish, griefe
§ aigre, sharpe, sower,
akecorne, (k) fruit
alacritie, chéerefulnes, liuelines
alablaster, (k) stone
alarum, a sound to the battell.

B 3   alchi-

An Alphabeticall table

alchimie, the art of turning other mettals into gold.
§ alien, a stranger
§ alienate, to estrange, or withdrawe the mind, or to make a thing another mans.
all haile, salute
alledge, bring proofe
allegation, alledging
allegorie, (gr) similitude, a misticall speech, more then the bare letter-
§ allegiance, obedience of a subiect
allienate, asswage, or make more easie and light
§ alliance, kindred, or league.
allusion, meaning and pointing to another matter then is spoken in words
allude, to speake one thing that hath resemblance and respect to another,
aliment, nourishment, sustenance
alpha, (gr) the first Greeke letter
alphabet, (g) order of letters in the crosserow.
altercation, debate, wrangling, or contention
altitude, height
amaritude, bitternesse
ambage, long circumstance of words.
§ ambassa-

## of hard English words.

§ ambassadour, messenger
ambition, desire of honour, or striuing for preferment
ambodexter, one y playeth on both hands.
ambiguous, doubtfull, vncertaine
§ ambushment, priuie traine, lying secretly to intrap by the way
§ amerce, } fine, or
amercement, } penalty.
amiable, louely, or with a good grace.
amitie, friendship, loue.
amorous, full of loue, amiable.
§ amorte, dead, extinguished, without life.
amplifie, enlarge, or make bigger.
analogie, (gr) conuenience, proportion.
analisis, (gr) resolution, deuiding into parts.
anarchie, (gr) when the land is without a prince, or gouernour.
anatomie, (g) cutting vp of the body.
anathema, (g) accursed or giuen ouer to the deuill.
anchoue, (k) of fruite.
§ angle, corner.
§ anguish, griefe.
angust, straight, narrow.
animate, encourage.

animauersion,

An Alphabeticall table

animaduersion, noting, considering, or marking.
annalis, chronicles of things from yeare to yeare.
annex, to knit or ioyne together.
annihilate, make voyd, or bring to nothing.
anniuersarie, a yeares minde, or done and comming yearely.
annuall, yearely.
anthem, song.
antecessor, an auncestour, or predecessour that goeth or liueth in the age or place before vs.
antichrist, (g) against, or contrarie to Christ.
anticipation, preuenting by a foreknowledge.
antidote, (g) a counterpoise, or remedy against poyson.
§ antidate, a fore date.
antipathie, (g) contrarietie of qualities.
antiquitie, auncientnes.
anticke, disguised.
antithesis (g) a repugnancie, or contrarietie.
antiquarie, a man skilled, or a searcher of antiquities.

annotations,

## of hard English words.

annotations, briefe doctrines or instructions.
anxitie, care or sorrow.
aphorisme, (g) generall rule in phisick.
apocalipse, (g) reuelation.
apocrypha (g) not of authoritie, a thing hidden, whose originall is not knowne.
apologie (g) defence, or excuse by speech.
apostotate (g) a backslider.
apostacie (g) falling away, backslyding, rebellion.
apostle (g) an ambassadour, or one sent.
apothegme (g) short wittie sentence, or speech.
apparant, in sight, or open.
appall, feare.
apparition, appearance, or strange sight.
§ appeach, accuse, or bewray.
§ appeale, to seeke to a higher Iudge.
§ appease, quiet, or pacifie.
appendix, hanging, or belonging to another thing.
appertinent,     ⎫ belonging vnto another
appurtenance, ⎭ thing.
appetite, desire to any thing.
applaude, to shew a liking of, as it were by clapping of hands.

application,

## An Alphabeticall table.

application, applying too, or resorting to
appose, to aske questions, oppose.
apposition, adding or setting too.
apprehension, conceite, and vnderstanding.
approbation, allowance, or liking.
appropriate, to take, and keepe to, and for himselfe alone.
approue, alowe, or make good.
approch, come nigh.
apt, fit
arbiter,     ⎫ a Judge in a controuersie
arbitratour, ⎭ betwixt men.
§ arbitrement, iudgement, censure, award.
arch, (g) chiefe.
arch-angell, (g) chiefe angell
archbishop, chiefe bishop
architest, chiefe builder.
ardent, hoate, earnest
ardencie, heate, earnestnes
argent, siluer, coyne
argue, to reason
ariditie, drinesse
aristocraticall, (g) gouernement of a kingdome by the peares and nobility.
arithmeticke, (g) art of numbring

arke,

## of hard English words.

arke, shippe or chest
§ armorie, house of armour
§ arrerages, debt vnpaid, or things left vndone and duties comming behind.
arrest, stay, or lay hold of
arride, to please well, to content
§ ariue, ⎱ come to land,
ariuall, ⎰ or approch.
arrogate, to claime, or challenge
arrogant, proude, presumptuous.
artifice, skill, subtiltie : or a cunning péece
 of worke
artificer, handicrafts-man
artificially, workmanlike, cunningly
articulate, ioynted, set together, or to point
 out, and distinguish
artichock, (k) herbe
§ artillery, engines or instruments for war.
ascend, goe vp, or clime vp
ascent, a going vp
ascribe, giue to, adde to, attribute onto
askey, ⎱ looking aside,
asquint, ⎰ or awry.
§ assay, proofe, or a triall :
assent, agréement, or consent
assertaine, assure : certaine
assentation, flattery : speaking faire

aspect,

# An Alphabeticall table

aspect, looking vpon, beholding much, sight
aspectable, worthie, or easie to be seene.
asperat, rough, sharpe, or vnpleasant.
asperation, breathing.
aspire, climbe vp, or come to, or high.
§ assault,   ⎱ to set vpon, or
§ assaile,   ⎰ to proue.
§ assemble, gather together.
assemblie, companie
assent, consent.
assertion, affirming, auouching of any thing
asseueration, earnest affirming
assiduitie continuance, diligence
assigne, appoint, ordaine
assignation, appointment.
assimulate, to make like, to compare with.
assistance, helpe
association, ioyning together in fellowship.
associate, to accompanie, or follow
§ assoyle, excuse, cleare
astipulation, an auouching, or witnessing of a thing, an agreement
astrictiue,  ⎱ binding, or ioyning
astringent,  ⎰ together.
astronomie, (g)  ⎱ knowledge of
astrologie, (g)   ⎰ the starres.
astrolabe, (g)

## of hard English words.

astrolabe, (g) an instrument to know the motion of the starres.

atheist, (g) ⎱ without, God, or beleeuing
atheall, ⎰ that there is no God, or denying any of his attributes.

atheisme, (g) the opinion of the atheist.

§ attach, sease vpon, rest, or hold

§ attaint, conuict of crime

§ attainder, a conuiction, or prouing guiltie of a crime or fault.

§ attempt, set vpon, or take in hand

attendance, watching, staying for, or wayting vpon.

attentiue, heedie, or marking

attenuate, to make thinner or weaker

attest, to witnesse, or call to witnesse

attrap, ensnare

attribute, giue to, or impute.

auarice, couetousnes, or inordinate desire of money.

auburne (k) colour

audience, hearing, or hearkening, or those that heare.

audacious, bold, rash, or foolish hardie

auditor, hearer, or officer of accounts

audible, easie to be heard.

auer, auouch, call to witnes, proue.

auert, to turne from, oz kéepe away.
augment, to encreafe
auguration, gueſſing, oz coniecturing at things to come:
§ avowable, ẏ which may be allowed and affirmed
§ avouch, affirme with earneſt, defend.
auoke, to call from, oz pull back
auſtere, ſharpe, rough, cruell
authenticall, (g) of authoʒitie, allowed by authoʒitie: the oʒiginall
autumne, the harueſt
axiome (g) a certaine pzinciple, oz general ground of any Art:
ay, euer, at any time, foz euer
azure, (k) of colour.

# B

BAile, furetie, witnes.
ballance, a paire of ſcales, oz other thing.
§ balaſe, grauell, wherewith ſhips are poyſed to goe vpʒight: oz weight.
bang, beat
bankerupt, bankerout, waſter
banquet, feaſt.

baptiſme,

## of hard English words.

baptisme, (g) dipping, or sprinkling.
§ band, company of men, or an assembly.
baptist, a baptiser
barbarian, a rude person
barbell, (k) fish
barbarie, (k) of fruite
barbarisme, barbarousnes, rudenes
§ barke, small ship
barnacle, (k) bird
barrester, one allowed to giue counsell, or to pleade:
barreter, a contentious person, quarreller, or fighter:
§ barter, to bargaine, or change
baud, whore
bauin, a faggot, or kid
bashfull, blush, or shamefast
§ battrie, beating or striking
bay, (k) tree.
beadle, office
beagle, (k) hound
beatitude, blessednes, happines
beldam, parent, or maister:
bellona, the goddesse of warre
benediction, praysing or blessing
beneficiall, profitable
beneuolence, good will, or fauour.
benigne,

An Alphabeticall table

benigne, fauourable, curteous, gentle:
benignitie, gentlenes, or kindnes
§ benisson, blessing
bequeath, giue:
bereft, depriued, alone, voide, robd.
besiedge, compasse
betrothed, affianced, or promised in mar=
　　riage:
bewaile, mone, complaine
§ biere, a cophin wherein dead men are
　　carried:
bigamie, (g) twise maried, or hath had two
　　wiues
billiment, iewell, or garment
bipartite, deuided into two parts
bisket, bread:
bishop, ouer-seer, or prelate
blase, report, publish, shew forth
blaspheme, (g) to speake ill of God:
blattering, vaine babling
§ blanch, to make white, or white lime
bleate, cry
blisse, ioy, or happines.
§ bonnet, hat, or cap.
bob, beate
§ bouge, stirre, remoue from a place.
boate, ship
　　　　　　　　　　　　　　　braule,

## of hard English words.

braule, wrangle.
brachygraphie, (g) short writing.
§ bragard, fine, trim, proude
§ brandish, to shake a sword
breuitie, shortnes
brickle, } easiely broken,
brittle, } lymber.
§ brigand, a theefe, or robber by the high way side.
§ brigandine, coate of defence
§ brigantine, a small ship
brothell, keeper of a house of baudry,
brooch, iewell.
§ bruite, report, noyse.
buggerie, coniunction with one of the same kinde, or of men with beasts.
bugle, glasse
buglasse, (k) herbe
bullyon, coyne
§ burgesse, a head man of a towne.

## C

CAlamitie, trouble, affliction.
   calcinate, to make salt:
calefie, make warme, heate, or chafe.
calygraphie, (g) fayre writing.
         C.        calli-

An Alphabeticall table

calliditie, craftines, or deceit
calumniation, a discrediting by worde, or false accusation.
camphire, kind of herbe.
capacitie, largenes of a place: conceit, or receiet.
§ capuchon, a hood
§ cancell, to vndoe, deface, crosse out, or teare
canon (g) law, or rule
canonise, (g) make a saint, to examine by rule:
canopie, couer
capitall, deadly, or great, or woorthy of shame, and punishment:
capable, wise, apt to learne, bigge, or fit to receiue.
capitulation, distinguishing by parts
captious, catching, deceitfull, subtile,
captiue, prisoner
captiuate, make subiect, or a prisoner,
cardinall, chiefe, or principall
carminate, to card wooll, or deuide
carnalitie, fleshlines
carnall, fleshly, pleasing the flesh:
carpe, take exception against, or wrangle.

cassere,

## of hard English words.

§ cassere, dismisse, put away, or out of office.

casualtie, chaunce or hap

castigation, chastisement, blaming, correction.

catalogue, (g) beadroole, or rehearesall of words, or names

category, (g) an accusation

catechiser, that teacheth the principles of Christian religion.

cathedrall, church, cheife in the diocesse

catharre, a flowing of humors from the head.

catholicke, (g) uniuersall or generall.

cauill, to iest, scoffe, or reason subtilly

caution, warning, putting in minde, or taking heede

celebrate, holy, make famous, to publish, to commend, to keepe solemlie

celeritie, swiftnes, hast

celestiall, heauenly, diuine passing excellent.

cement, morter, or lime.

censor, a corrector, a iudge, or reformer of manners

censure, correction, or reformation

centre, (g) middest of any round thing

An Alphabeticall table
or circle.

centurion, captaine of a hundred men.
ceruse, white leade, or painting that women vse.
cessement, tribute
chanell, sinke:
character, (g) the fashion of a Letter, a marke, or stampe:
§ chaunt, sing
§ champion, wilde field, also a challenger,
chambering, lightnes, and wanton behauiour in priuate places
charter, a grant of any thing confirmed by seale.
§ cheualrie, knight-hood
cherubin, order of Angels:
chibball, (k) fruite
chirograph, (g) hand writing
chiromancie (g) telling of fortunes, by the lines in the hands:
chirurgion, (g) a surgion
choller, (gr) a humor causing anger
chough, (k) bird:
christ, (g) annointed
chronickler, (g) ⎫ historie wri-
chronographer, ⎭ ter.
chronicall, (g) returning at certaine times

chro-

## of hard English words.

chronologie, (g) storie of times past.
cibaries, meates, nourishment
cider, drinke made of apples
circuit, about.
circumcise, to cut the priuie skin
circumference, the round and outmost circuit, or compasse
circumligate, binde about
circumscribe, to cōpasse about with a line, to limit.
circumspect, heedie, quicke of sight, wise, and doing matters aduisedly.
circumlocution, a speaking of that in many words, which may be said in few
circumstance, a qualitie, that accompaneth any thing, as time, place, &c
circumstant, things that are about us,
circumuent, to close in, to deceaue, or intrap craftily.
citron, (k) fruit
ciuilitie, honest in conuersation, or gentle in behauiour.
clamarus, making a great noyse
classick, chiefe, and approued,
§ clauicordes, mirth,
claritude, clærenes, renowne,
clemencie, gentlenes, curtesie.
client,

An Alphabeticall table

client, he that is defended.
climate, a portion of the worlde betwixt north and south
climactericall, (g) that which ariseth by degrees, as the sixtie third yeere is climactericall of seauentie.
clister, medicine
coble, amend
coadiutor, a fellow helper.
cockatrice, a kind of beast
cœnation, supper, or a place to sup in
cogitation, thought, musing
cognition, knowledge
cohærence, ioyning, a vniting together.
§ coin, corner
collect, gather together
colleague, companion,
collaterall, on the other side, ouer against, as two lines drawne equally distant one from another, in due place
collation, recitall, a short banquet
collect, gather
collusion, deceit, cousanage
colume, one side of a page of a booke
combine, heale, or couple together,
cōbination, a ioyning, or coupling together
combure, burne, or consume with fire

com-

## of hard English words.

combustible, easily burnt
combustion, burning or consuming with fire.
comedie, (k) stage play,
comicall, handled merily like a comedie
commemoration, rehearsing or remembring
§ cōmencement, a beginning or entrance
comet, (g) a blasing starre
comentarie, exposition of any thing
commerce, fellowship, entercourse of merchandise.
commination, threatning, or menacing,
commiseration, pittie
commodious, profitable, pleasant, fit,
commotion, rebellion, trouble, or disquietnesse.
communicate, make partaker, or giue part vnto
§ communaltie, common people, or common-wealth
communion, ⎱ fellow-
communitie, ⎰ ship.
compact, ioyned together, or an agrǣmēt.
compassion, pitty, fellow-feeling
compell, to force, or constraine
compendious, short, profitable

com-

## An Alphabeticall table

compensation, a recompence:
compeare, like
competent, conuenient, sufficient, apt:
competitor, hee that sueth for the same thing, or office, that another doth:
compile, gather together
complement, perfecting of any thing
complet, fulfilled, finished
Complexion, nature, constitution of the body.
§ complices, fellowes in wicked matters
compose, make, or ioyne together
composition, agreement, a making, or mingling together.
comprehend, ⎫ to con-
comprise,   ⎭ taine.
comprimise, agreement, made by parties chosen on either side
comprimit, iudge
compte, fine, decked: trimmed
compulsion, force, constraint
computation, an account or reckoning
compunction, pricking
concauitie, hollownes
conceale, to keepe close
conception, conceiuing in the wombe.
concinnate, made fit, finely apparelled

concise,

## of hard English words.

concise, briefe or short
concoct, to digest meate
concord, ⎱ agree-
concordance, ⎰ ment.
concrete, ioyned, or congealed together
concruciate, to torment, or vex together
concubine, harlot, or light huswife.
conculcate, to treade vnderfoote
concupiscence, desire
concurre, agree together, runne together, or meete.
concurse, running together of many to a place.
condigne, worthie
condiscende, agree vnto, or consent
condole, to be greeued, or sorrowfull with another.
conduct, guiding, or hiring
confabulate, to talke together
confection, compounding, making, or mingling.
confederate, agreeing peaceably together by couenants made
conferre, talke together
conference, communication, talking together.
confidence, trust, hope

confine,

## An Alphabeticall table

confine, to border vpon, to compasse in
confirme, establish
§ confiscation, forfeiture or losse of goods
conflict, battaile, strife, fight
conforme, to make like vnto, consent
confound, ouerthrow, destroy, mingle together, or disorder.
§ confront, oppose, compare one to another.
congeale, to harden, or waxe hard, or freeze together
congestion, a heaping vp
conglutinate, to ioyne together
congratulate, to reioyce with another for some good fortune.
congregate, gather together
congruence, ⎱ agreablenes,
congruitie,  ⎰ or likenes.
coniunction, ioyning together
coniure, to conspire together, to sweare by.
connexion, ioyning together
conniuence, sufferance, or winking at
conquest, a complayning, or victorie
consanguinitie, kinred by blood, or birth
consecrate, make holie, to dedicate, or giue vnto.

consectarie,

## of hard English words.

consectarie, one that followeth any opinion.
consent, agreement
consequence, ⎱ following
consequent, ⎰ by order.
conserue, keepe, saue, or maintaine
consideratly, wisely, and with aduise, consist, stand
§ consistorie, place of ciuill iudgement
consociate, companie with, or ioyne a companion vnto.
consolation, comfort
consonant, agreeable, likelie
consort, a companion, or company
conspicuous, easie to be seene, excellent
conspire, agree together, for to doe euill.
constellation, a company of starrs
constitutions, lawes, or decrees
construe, expound
consul, a chiefe gouernor among the Romanes.
consult, take counsaile
consumate, accomplish, fulfill, or finish.
contagious, that which corrupteth, or infecteth.
contaminate, defiled, or corrupted
contaminouse, infectious, defiled
contemplation,

contemplation, meditation, or musing
contend, wrangle
contestate, to call to witnes
context, the agreeing of the matter going before, with that which followeth.
continent, modest, abstaining, chast: also the firme land where no ile or sea is.
contingent, happening by chaunce
contract, make short, also a bargaine, or couenant.
contradiction, gaine saying
contribute, bestowe vpon, or giue vnto
contribution, a bestowing of any thing
contributorie, giuing a part to any thing
contrite, broken, sorrowfull
contrition, sorrow, sadnes
contriue, make
contumacie, stubbornnes, contempt
contumelie, slaunder, reproch
contusion, bruised, or beaten
conuent, bring before a iudge
conuenient, fit, well beseeming
conuenticle, a little assemblie
conuerse, companie with
conuert, turne, change
conuict, proued guiltie, ouercome
conuince, to ouercome, confute, or proue manifestly.

## of hard English words.

manifestly.
conuocation, an assembling, or calling together.
§ conuoy, a waiting vppon: or keeping company in the way.
connulsion, a pulling, or shrinking vp
copartner, fellow partaker, or companion
cophin, (g) basket, or chest for a dead body to be put in.
copious, plentifull, abounding
copulation, ioyning, or coupling together
cordwainer, shoemaker, or trade
cordiall, comforting the hart.
§ coriuals, competitors
carnositie, full of flesh, grosse
corporall, bodily
corporate, hauing a bodie:
§ corps, deade bodie
corpulent, grosse of body, fat, or great
correspondent, answerable
correllatiues, when 2. things are so linked together, that the one cannot be without the otherr.
corrigible, easily corrected
corroborate, confirme, or strengthen, or make strong.
corroded, gnawd about

corrosiue,

An Alphabeticall table

corrosiue, fretting
cosmographie, (g) description of the world.
costiue, bound in the bodie
§ couch, bed, lie downe:
§ couert, hidden place, secrete
§ counterchange, to change againe:
§ countermaund, commaund contrarie
§ countermine, vndermine one against another.
§ countermure, to builde, one wall against another.
crassitude, fatnesse or thicknesse
§ counterpoise, make leuell, or to weigh, as heuie as another thing.
cowslip, (k) hearb
§ counteruaile, of equall valew
credence, beliefe
§ curbe, restraine, keepe in:
credible, which may be beleeued
§ couerture, couering
creditor, he which lendeth, or trusteth another:
credulous, readie to belieue, true
credulitie, rashnes in belieuing
§ creuas, rift.
§ crible, sifted

criminous,

## of hard English words.

criminous, ⎫ faultie, that wherein is some
criminall, ⎭ fault.
crisped, curled, or frisled.
criticall, (g) which giueth iudgement of sicknes. &c.
crocodile, (k) beast
crucifie, fasten to a crosse
crude, raw, not ripe, not digested:
crupt, (g) hidden, or secret
crystaline, (g) cleere like glasse, or chrystall.
cubite, a foote and a halfe
culpable, blame-worthy, guiltie,
culture, husbandry, tilling
curiositie, picked diligence, greater carefulnes, then is seemely or necessarie,
cursorilie, swiftly, or briefely.
curuefie, bowed, or made crooked.
custodie, keeping, or looking to
cymball, an instrument of musicke, so called.
cynicall, (g) doggish, froward.
cypher, (g) a circle in numbering, of no value of it selfe, but serueth to make vp the number, and to make other figures of more value.

Damna-

## D

Amnable, not to be allowed.
deacon, (g) prouider for the poore
demonaicke, (g) possessed with a deuill.
deambulation, a walking abroade
§ debate, strife, contention
debar, let:
debilitie, weakenes, faintnes.
§ debonnayre, gentle, curteous, affable,
decalogue, (g) the ten commaundements:
decacordon, (g) an instrument with tenne strings
decent, comlie, or beséeming
decease, a departing, or giuing place to.
decide, to determine, or make an end of.
decipher, describe, or open the meaning, or to count.
decision, cutting away.
declamation, an oration of a matter feyned.
decline, fall away, or swarue from,
decoction, liquor, wherein things are sod for phisicke.
decorum, comlines
decrepite, very old
dedicate, to giue for euer.

deduct,

## of hard English words.

deduct, take or drawe out, abate, or diminish.
§ deface, blot out, staine, bring out of fashion
defame, to slaunder, or speake ill of
defect, want, fayling
§ defie, distrust.
define, to shew clearely what a thing is.
deflower, dishonest, rauish, or disgrace
deformed, ill shapen, ill fauored
§ defraude, deceiue, beguile
§ defraye, lay out, pay, discharge
degenerate, be vnlike his auncestours: to grow out of kind.
dehort, mone or perswade from, to aduise to the contrarie.
deitie, Godhead
deifie, make like God
delectation, delight, or pleasure
delegate, an imbassadour, or one appointed in anothers place.
deliberate, to take good counsell
delineate, to drawe the proportion of any thing.
delicate, daintie, giuen to pleasure
delude, deceiue, or laugh to scorne.
§ deluge, great floode, or ouer flowing of waters:

An Alphabeticall table
waters.
delusion, mockerie, a deceitfull thing
demaund, request, aske
demerite, deseruing, worthines
democracie, (g) a common-wealth gouerned by the people.
demonstrate, shew plainely, or openly, to point out or manifest.
demenour, behauiour
§ demurre, to stay, to linger, or vse delaies
denison, free borne
denounce, declare, or giue warning of, or proclaime
denomination, a naming
depend,       ⎱ hang
dependance,  ⎰ vpon.
deplore, to lament or bewaile
deplume, to pull of the feathers
deportation, carrying away
depopulate, spoile, or wast
depose, put away, depriue, or put downe.
dapraue, marre or corrupt, or make worse.
deprecation, supplication, or requiring of pardon
depresse, to keepe downe
depriue, see depose
depute, account, or esteeme

deride,

of hard English words.

deride, mock, or laugh to scorne.
derision, mocking
deriue, fetch from
deriuation, taking away from some other matter.
derogate, to take away, or to diminish
§ desastrous, vnluckie, vnfortunate
descend, goe downe.
describe, to write foorth, to copie out, or to declare
§ deseigne,        ⎰ an appoynting how any
§ deseignment, ⎱ thing shall be done.
desert, wildernesse.
desertion, a leauing, or forsaking
designe, to marke out, or appoint for any purpose:
desist, leaue off, or stay
desolate, left alone, or forsaken
desperate, without hope, or past hope,
detect, bewray, disclose, accuse
destinated, appointed,
destitute, forsaken
detest, hate greatly, or abhorre
deteined, withholden, or kept back,
determine, resolue, conclude
detract, take from, or backbite
detriment, losse or hurt

D 2                    detrude,

detrude, thrust out, or from
deuote, to giue vnto, or appoint vnto
deuotion, holinesse.
§ deuoyre, dutie
dexteritie, aptnes, nimblenes
diabolicall, (g) deuilish.
diademe, (g) a Kings crowne:
diapason, (g) a concorde in musick of all parts
diet, manner of foode
dialect, the manner of speech in any language, diuers from others.
dialogue (g) conference, or talking together.
diameter, (g) a line, crossing the midst of any circle or figure
didacticall, (g) full of doctrine or instruction.
diffamation, a slaundering, or speaking ill of:
different, vnlikely, disagreeing,
difficill,   } hard, vneasie,
difficult,   } dangerous
diffident, mistrustfull
diffude, poure out
digest, bring into order, to deuide, & distribute things into their right place.

dignity,

## of hard English words.

dignitie, worthinesse
digresse, turne from, goe away
digression, departing from the matter in hand
dilacerate, to rent in sunder:
dilate, enlarge, spread abroade, or to discourse vpon largely
dilemma, (g) a forked kinde of argument, which on either side entrappeth.
dimension, measuring
diminution, lessening
diocesse, (g) iurisdiction
diocesan, that hath iurisdiction
direct, guide, or rule: right, straight, also to order.
disable, make vnable, or finde fault with.
disabilitie, vnablenes
§ disaduantageous, hindering much
disanull, make voyde, or bring to nothing.
§ disburse, lay out money
discent, comming downe from another
discerne, know, put one from another, or put difference
discide, cut off, or in peeces
discipline, instruction, or training vp.
disciple, scholler,
discipher, to lay open, or make plaine

## An Alphabeticall table

disclose, discouer, vtter, or manifest.

§ discomfiting, putting to flight

discord, disagræment, variance

discretion, wise choise of one from another

discusse, examine, debate, or search narrowly into:

disfigure, bring out of shape,

§ disfranchis, take away frædome:

disioyne, vnioyne, or seperate

disiunction, a deuiding, or seperating,

§ disfranchised, depriued of libertie.

disgrade, to discharge of his orders, or degrées.

§ disguised, counterfeited, seeming that it is not:

dislocation, setting out of right place,

§ disloyall, one whō it is not good to trust, vntrustie, traytetous.

dismember, to pull and part one péece from another.

dismisse, let passe, or send away

disparagement, hurt, hinderance, or disgrace:

dispence, to giue licence vnto

disperse, scatter, or spread abroade.

dispeople, to vnpeople a place

displant, to pull vp by the rootes, trées planted.

## of hard English words.

planted,
display, spread abroade
dispose, to set in order, to appoint.
disposition, naturall inclination, or setting in order.
dispoyle, take away by violence, or rob
disputable, questionable, or doubtfull, that may be reasoned of:
dissent, disagree, to be of a contrarie opinion.
dissimilitude, vnlikenes
dissimulation, dissembling
dissipation, scattering abroade
dissolue, vnloose, or melte
dissoluble, easie to vnloose
dissolute, carelesse, rechlesse
dissolution, breaking, vnloosing.
dissonant, disagreeing
distance, space betwæne
distended, stretched out, or out of ioynt.
distinguish, put difference, deuide, or point out from others.
distillation, ⎫ dropping downe by
distilling,   ⎭ little and little.
distinct, differing, or deuided
distinction, a difference, or seperation
distracted, drawne into diuerse parts

distribute,

### An Alphabeticall table

distribute, deuide in sunder, or to giue in
  sundric parts.
distribution, diuision, or laying out by
  parts.
disturbe, disquiet, let, or interrupt
disswade, to perswade to the contrarie
dittie, the matter of a song.
diuert, turne from, to another
diuine, Heauenly godly, also to gesse, con-
  iecture, or prophesie.
diuinitie, heauenly, doctrine, also godhead.
diuision, parting, or seperating
diurnall, a daily mouing
divulgate, publish, or make common
docilitie, easie to be taught
doctrine, learning, or instruction
dolor, griefe, sorow, or paine
dolorous, grieuous, or sorrowfull
§ domage, losse, harme, or hinderance
domesticall, at home, belonging to houshold: priuate
dominere, rule, beare sway
domicilles, houses
dominion,     } rule, lordship or
domination,  } maistership.
donatiue, a gift, in money or other things
dulcimur,

## of hard English words.

dulcimur, } (k) instru-
dulcimar,  } ment.
duarchy, the equall raigne of two princes together.
driblets, small debts
dulcifie, sweeten
dulcor, sweetnesse
durable, long lasting, or of long continuance.

## E

Ebullient, seething
ebulliated, boyled
clipse, (g) failing of the light of the sunne or moone
eccho, a sound, resounding back againe
ecclesiasticall, (g) belonging to the church
eden, pleasure, or delight
edict, a commaundement from authoritie, a proclamation.
edifice, building
edifie, instruct, or builde up in knowledge.
edition, putting foorth, setting abroade
education, bringing up
effect, a thing done, or to bring to passe

effectuall,

## An Alphabeticall table.

effectuall, forcible

effeminate, womannish, delicate, wanton.

efficacie, force, or strength

efficient, working, or accomplishing

effusion, powring, or running foorth

eglogue, (g) a talking together

egresse, foorthgoing, or passage out

eiection, a casting foorth

elaborate, done curiously and dilligently.

election, choise

elect, chosen, or picked out

elegancie, finesse of speech

element, the first principle or beginning of any thing.

elench, (g) a subtill argument

eleuate, lift vp, or heaue vp

elocution, good vtterance of speech.

emerods, (k) of disease

§ embark,  ⎱ to ship a thing, or
imbark,    ⎰ load a ship.

emblem, (g) a picture shadowing out some thing to be learned.

eminent, appearing, higher, or further out, excelling.

emmot, pismire

emphasis, (g) a forcible expressing

§ empire,

## of hard English words.

§ empire, gouernement: or kingdome
emulation, enuie, or imitate
enarration, declaration, expounding
enigmaticall, (g) full of hard questions, obscure.
§ enchaunt, bewitch
encounter, set against, or to meete
§ encrochment, when the Lord hath gotten seisen of more rent, or seruices of his tenant then of right is due.
§ endosse, cut on the back, or write on the back.
enduce, moue
enimitie, ⎱ displeasure, or
enmitie,  ⎰ hatred.
enflame, burne, or set on fire.
§ enfranchise, make free
§ engrate, presse vpon
§ enhaunce, to lift vp, or make greater:
§ enlarge, make bigger, set at libertie
§ enoble, make noble, or famous
enormious, out of square, vnorderly
§ ensigne, flagge for war
§ enterlace, to put betwéene, intermingle:
§ enterprise, beginne, take in hand
§ enterre, lay in the earth
§ entrals, inward parts, as hart, liuer, &c.

§ enuiron,

## An Alphabeticall table

§ enuiron, to enclose, or compasse about.
epha, kind of measure
epicure, giuen to pleasure.
epigram, (g) a sentence, written vpon any for praise, or dispraise
epilogue, (g) conclusion
epilepsis, (g) the falling sicknes
episcopall, (g) bishoplike.
epiphanie, (g) appearing
epitaph, (g) the writing on a tombe or graue.
epithite, (g) a name or title giuen to any thing.
epitome, (g) the briefe copie of a booke, &c.
epitomise, (g) to make an epitome, or to bring a booke into a lesser volume.
equalize, match, or make equall
equinoctium, when the dayes and nights are equall.
§ equipage, furniture
equitie, right, lawfulnes
erect, set vp, or lift vp
equiualent, of equall valew.
ermite, (g) one dwelling in the wildernes.
erronious, full of errour, and wandring out of the right way.
§ essay, tryall what one can say, or doe in

any

## of hard English words

any matter.
§ escheat, forfaite
§ eschew, shunning, auoyde, escape
§ espoused, promised in marriage
essence, substance, or being of any thing
§ essoine, excused for any cause
§ establish, confirme, make strong
estimate, esteeme, value, or prise, thinke or iudge.
eternall, euerlasting, without end
ethnick, (g) an heathen, or gentile
etymologie, (g) true expounding
euacuated, made voyde, cleane taken away: or emptied.
euangell, (g) the gospell: or glad tidings
euangelist, (g) bringer of glad tidings
euaporate, to breath out
euent, chaunce, or that which followeth any thing.
euict, ouercome by law
eucharist, (g) a thanksgiuing, the Lords supper.
eunuch, (g) gelded, wanting stones
euert, turne vpside downe
euident, easie to be seene, plaine
euocation, calling forth
exact, perfectly done, or to require with extremitie.

An Alphabeticall table

extremitie.
exaggerate, heape vpon, amplifie to make a thing more then it is
exaltation, lifting vp
exasperate, whet on, to vex, or make more angrie
excauate, make hollow
excæcate, to make blind
excessiue, too much, more then enough
§ excheaquer, office of receits
exclaime, bray, or crie out
exclude, thrust, or shut out, or keepe out
excogitate, to muse, or deuise exactly.
excommunicate, to thrust out of company, or fellowship
excrement, dung, offall, refuse, or dregs.
excruciat, to vex, or torment
excursion, a skirmidh in warres, of some few running from their companie
execrable, cursed
execute, performe, or exercise some charge
exempt, free, priuiledged.
exemplifie, enlarge, or declare by examples

exhalation,

## of hard English words.

exhalation, a breath, or fume rising vpward
exhaust, drawne out, or emptied
exhibite, put vp or bestow : to offer, or set abroade for all men to see
exiccate, to drie vp
exile, banish, driue out
exorable, easie, to be intreated
exorbitant, out of order, measure or place.
exorcist, (g) coniurer
§ exorde, beginne
exordium, a beginning, or entrance
expect, looke for
expedient, fit, meete or beseeming
expedition, hast, speede
expell, put out, or thrust out
expend, consider, or muse vpon
expence, cost, or money layd out
experiment, a proofe, or triall
expert, skilfull
expiation, pacifying with satisfaction, purging by sacrifice
expire, to die, or giue vp the ghost to decay.
explane, to make manifest, or declare
explicate, declare plainely
§ exploit, enterprise, act, deede

expose,

## An Alphabeticall table

expose, to offer, or lay open, to hazard,
expostulate, to reason, or chide with, to complaine:
expresly, fitly, manifestly
exprobration, vpbreyding, casting in ones teeth.
expugnable, to be wonne, or ouercome.
expulse, driue out, or thrust out
exquisite, perfect, fine, singuler, curious.
extant, appearing, abroad, shewing it selfe.
extasie, a traunce, or sowning.
extemporall,⎫
extempore,   ⎬ suddaine, without premeditation, or studie.
extemporarie,⎭
extende, spread forth, prolong, or make longer, to inlarge.
extenuate, lessen, minish, or make lesse.
externall, outward, strange
extinguish, put out, or quench
extinct, put out
extirpate, to pull vp by the rootes
extoll, aduaunce, or praise highly, to lift vp
extort, to wring out, to wrest from by violence.
extract, drawne out
extrauagant, wandring out of order.
exulcerate, to make sore, to corrupt.
       Fabricate,

## F

Fabricate, make, fashion.
  fabulous, fained, counterfeited, much talked of
fact, deede
facilitie, easines
faction, deuision of people into sundry parts and opinions
factious, that maketh deuision, contentious.
factor, one that doth busines for another
facultie, licence, power, aptnes
fallacie, deceit, falshood
falsifie, to forge, or counterfait
fame, report, common talke, credite
fantacie, imagination
§ fantastique, conceited, full of deuises
§ farce, to fill, or stuffe
fascinate, to bewitch, or diffigure by inchauntment.
fastidiousnes, lothsomnesse, or disdainfullnesse
§ faschious, grieuous, or inducing to anger.
fatall, mortall, appointed by God to come

An Alphabeticall table
to paſſe.
§ fealtie, faithfulnes
fecunditie, fruitfulneſſe
felicitie, happineſſe
§ female,    ⎱ the ſhe in mankind, oꝛ other
feminine,   ⎰      creatures.
fermentated, leauened
feruide, hote, ſcalding, burning
feſtination, haſt, ſpeede
feſtiuitie, mirth, pleaſantnes
feſtiuall, merrie, pertaining to holy daies
feruent, hote, chafed, verie angrie
fertile, fruitfull, yeelding much fruit
feuer, ague
fiction, a lie, oꝛ tale fained
fidelitie, faithfulnes, truſtines
figurate, to ſhadowe, oꝛ repꝛeſent, oꝛ to
    counterfaite
figuratiue, by figures
finall, pertaining to the end
finite, hauing an end, and certaine limits.
firme, ſure, ſtedfaſt, ſtrong, conſtant
fixed, faſtned, ſure, faſt
§ flagon, great wine cup, oꝛ bottell
flagrant, burning, hot
flexible, eaſilie bent, pliant, oꝛ mutable
§ flote, ſwime aloft
                                        fluxible,

## of hard English words.

fluxible, thin, and running easily downe like water.
§ floscles, flowers
fluxe, disease of scouring
§ feeble, weake, lacking strength
fomentation, an asswaging, or comforting by warmth.
foraine, strange, of another country
formall, following the common fashion
foraminated, holed, or bored
formidable, fearefull, to be feared
fornication, uncleannes betweene single persones.
fortification, strengthning
fortitude, valiantnes, or couragiousnes, strength
fortunate, happie, hauing good successe
fragilitie, brittlenes, or weakenes
fragments, reliques, broken meates, peeces broken of.
fragrant, sweetly smelling
§ franck, liberall, bountifull
fraternitie, brotherhood
§ franchise, libertie, freedome
fraudulent, deceitfull, craftie, or ful of guile.
frequent, often, done many times: ordinarie, much haunted, or goe too.

## An Alphabeticall table

frigifie, coole, make cold
friuolous, vaine, trifeling, of no estimation.
frontlet, (k) attire for the fore-head
fructifie, to make fruitfull, or bring foorth much fruit.
frugall, thriftie, temperate in expences
fruition, inioying, possession
frustrate, make voyde, deceiue
fugitiue, runnagate, or starting away
fulgent, glistering, or shining
fuluide, yellowe
fume, to yeeld smoke
function, calling, or charge, or trade, and place wherein a man liueth.
funerall, buriall, mourning: pertaining to a buriall, or mourning.
furbush, to dresse or scoure, or make cleane
§ furniture, all things necessary to vse
furious, raging, or mad
future, that which shall be heereafter
§ garboile, hurlie burly
gardian, a keeper, or defendor
gargarise, to wash the mouth, and throate within, by stirring some liquor vp and downe in the mouth,
garnar, } corne, or corne
granar, } chamber.

§ garnish,

## of hard English words.

§ garnish, trime, deck vp, make fine.
gem, a precious stone
§ gaie, fine, trim
gentilitie, ⎱ gentrie, nobilitie,
generositie, ⎰ gentlemanship.
genesis, (g) beginning
gentile, a heathen
generation, offspring
genealogie, (g) generation, or a describing of the stock or pedegree.
genitalles, priuities
genuine, peculiar, or naturall
genius, the angell that waits on man, be it a good or euill angell
genitor, father
geographie, (g) the describing of the earth.
geometrie, (g) art of measuring the earth.
geomancie, (g) sorcerie by circkles, and pricks in the earth
germane, come of the same stock
gests, things done, or noble acts of princes
gibbocitie, crookednes
gire, grin, or laugh
giues, fetters
glee, mirth, gladnes
gospell, glad tidings
globe, any thing, very round.

G 3    glorifie,

## An Alphabeticall table

glorifie, to giue honour, praise, and commendation to any body.
gloſſe, a tongue, or expoſition of a darke speech.
gloze, diſſemble
§ gourmandiſe, deuouring, gluttony
glutinate, to glue, or ioyne together
gnible, bite
gnomen, (g) the ſtile, or cock of a diall
gradation, ſteps, by little and little.
graduate, that hath taken a degrée
gratifie, to pleaſure, or do a good turne in way of thankfulnes
gratis, frœly, without deſert
gratitude, thankfulnes
gratulate, to be glad for anothers ſake,
graue, waightie, ſober, ſage, diſcréete
greaſe, fat
§ guerdon, a reward:
§ guidance, gouerning, or direction
§ guiſe, faſhion, ſhape, cuſtome,
gulfe, déepe poole, or pit
guſtation, taſte

## H

Habilitie,  ⎱ ablenes, or of  
abilitie,   ⎰ ſufficiencie.

habi=

## of hard English words.

habitable, able to dwell in
habitacle, ⎫ a dwelling
habitation, ⎭ place:
habite, apparell, fashion, custome
habitude, disposition, plight, respect
§ hale, pull, draw, lift vp
halaluiah, praise the Lord
hallucinate, to deceiue, or blind
harmonie (g) agræement of diuers sounds in musicke.
§ hautie, loftie, proude
§ hazard, venture, chaunce:
§ herault, kings messenger
heathen, see Gentile
hebrew, from Hebers stock
hecticke, (g) inflaming the hart, and soundest parts of the bodie
hemisphere, (g) halfe of the compasse of heauen, that we see.
helmet, head peece,
hereditarie, cōming by inheritance, or succession.
heritage, inheritance, possession
herbinger, sent before to prepare
heriticall, (g) ⎫ one that maintaineth heresies.
hereticke, (g) ⎭
hermite, see ermite

heroi=

## An Alphabeticall table

heroicall, (g) beséeming a noble man, or magnificent:

§ hideous, fearefull, terrible

hierarchie, (g) the gouernment of priests, or holy gouernance:

hymne, (g) kinde of song to the prayse of GOD.

hipocrite, (g) such a one as in his outward apparrell, countenaunce, & behauiour, pretendeth to be another man, then he is indéede, or a deceiuer.

historicall, (g) pertaining to historie

§ homage, worship, or seruice.

§ homicide, a man killer, or the killing of a man:

hononimie, (g) whē diuers things are signified by one word

horror, fearefull sorrow, feare, terror.

horizon, (g) a circle, deuiding the halfe of the firmament, frō the other halfe which we sée not.

hosanna, saue now:

hospitality, good entertainement for friends and strangers.

§ hostage, pledge

hostilitie, hatred, or enmitie, or open wars.

huckster, marchant, or trade

humane,

## of hard English words

humane, belonging to man, gentle, curteous, bounteous.
humide, wet,
humiditie, moysture
huſh, ⎱ peace, or be
huſht, ⎰ still.
hyperbolicall, (g) beyond all credite, or likelihoode of truth.

### I

Idiome, (g) a proper forme or ſpeech:
idiot, (g) unlearned, a foole
Iehoua, Lord almighty
ientation, breakefaſt
ieoperdie, danger
Ieſus, Sauiour.
ignoble, of low and baſe birth
ignominie, reproch, diſcredite, ſlaunder.
illegitemate, unlawfully begotten, and borne.
illiquinated, unmelted
illiterate, unlearned, without knowledge.
illuſtrate, to make plaine, to declare
illuminate, to inlighten, or make plaine
illuſion, mockerie, ieſting, or ſcoffing
imbecilitie, weakenes, feeblenes

imbarge,

## An Alphabeticall table

imbarge, } sée em-
imbarke, } barke
imitation, following, doing the like:
immaculate, vnspotted, vndefiled
immanitie, beastlie, crueltie, or hugenesse and greatnes
immature, vnripe, or out of season:
immediate, next to, not hauing any other betwixt
imminent, at hand, ready to come vpon
immoderate, without measure, excéeding great, or excessiue
immortall, euerlasting, that dieth not
immunitie, frǽdome from any thing, or libertie:
immure, to shut vp, or inclose within wals
immutable, constant, still the same, vn-changable:
§ impart, to make partaker of, to tell to
impacience, lacke of sufferance
§ impaire, diminish, lessen
§ impeach, accuse, hurt, or hinder
impediment, let, or hinderance
impenetrable, that cannot be pierced, or entred into:
impenitent, vnrepentant:
imperated, commaunded, or ruled ouer

imperi-

## of hard English words.

imperious, desiring to rule, full of commaunding, stately
imperfection, vnperfectnes
imperiall, belonging to the crowne
impertinent, not pertaining to the matter.
impetrate, obtaine by request
impetuous, violent
impietie, vngodlines, crueltie
implacable, that cannot be pleased or pacified.
implement, stuffe:
imply, to signifie, or make manifest
imploy, bestow, spend
implore, to desire with teares,
implume, to pull off the feathers
impose, lay vpon, or put on
importance, of value, force, or worth:
§ impost, tribute
imposture, falshood, deceit,
impotent, weake, feeble,
importune, to be earnest with
importunate, requiring earnestly, without beeing satisfied, till the request be obteyned.
imprecation, cursing, or wishing euill vnto.
§ impregnable, vnuanquished, not able to be

An Alphabeticall table

be ouercome, strong.
impression, printing, marking, or stamping:
improper, vnfit, vnseemely, common
impropriation, a thing accounted poper, which is not indeede
improbable, that cannot be proued.
improuident, carelesse, not foreseeing, or taking heede before hand.
imprudent, ignorant, rash, carelesse:
impudent, shamelesse,
impugne, resist:
impunitie, lack, or omission of punishment
impuritie, filthines, vncleannesse, dishonestie.
impute, reckon, or assigne, blame, or to lay to ones charge
inabilitie, want of power or abilitie.
inamored, in loue with.
inaugurate, to aske counsell of soothsayers.
incarnate, taking flesh vpō him, or to bring flesh vpon.
incense, kind of offering made by fire
incend, kindle, burne, vexe, or chafe, to incense, to stirre vp, or to set on fire, or to anger.
incessantlie, earnestlie, without ceasing

incest,

## of hard English words.

incest, vnlawfull copulation of man and woman within the degrees of kinred, or alliance, forbidden by gods law, whether it be in marriage or otherwise.
inchaunt, bewitch, or charme
incident, happening, or chauncing
incision, cutting, in searching of a wound
incitate, to moue, or prouoke
incline, leane vnto, or towards
include, to shut in, or containe within
incommodious, hurtfull, vnfit
incommunicable, that cannot bee imparted to any other, or proper to one person, and none other.
incomperable, that hath not his like
incompatible, insufferable
incomprehensible, that cannot be conceiued, or vnderstood
incongruencie, want of agreement
inconsiderate, rash, not taking counsaile
incontinent, liuing loosely, or vnchastly
incontinently, presently, disorderly, or without moderation.
incredible, marueilous, such as cannot be beleeued.
incorporate, to graft one thing into the bodie of another, to make one bodie or substance

An Alphabeticall table

stance of two or moe, to mixe or put together.
incorruptible, vncorruptible, vnperishable, or not subiect to corruption
incredulous, hardly brought to beleeue
inculcate, to vrge, or repeate one thing often:
inculpable, without fault, blamelesse,
incurable, past cure, a wound that cannot be healed:
incur, runne into
indecent, not comly, or beseeming,
indeere, make bound to one,
indefinite, without rule, or order, not determined:
indemnitie, without losse
indignitie, vnworthinesse, vnseemly vsage, infamie, or disgrace
indignation, anger, chafing,
indissoluble, that cannot be vnloosed or vndone:
¶ indite, to signifie, or giue in ones name.
induce, to moue vnto, or allure, or draw:
indulgence, sufferance, too gentle intreating.
induction, bringing in
indurate, harden.

industrie,

## of hard English words.

industrie, diligence or labour
ineffable, vnspeakable, y cannot be vttered
inequalitie, vnlikenes
inestimable, that cannot be valued, or accounted of as it deserueth.
ineuitable, that cannot be auoyded.
inexorable, that cannot, or will not be intreated to graunt
infallible, vndeceiueable, vnguilefull, trustie.
infamous, ill reported of, or defamed
infatuate, to make foolish.
infection, corrupting
infernall, belonging to hell,
inferre, bring in, to alleage, or signifie
infidelitie, vnfaithfulnes:
infinite, without number, or end
infirmitie, weakenes:
inflamation, inflaming, or setting on fire
inflexible, that cannot be bended, vnruly.
inflict, to lay vpon
influence, a flowing in.
informe, giue notice to teach, to beginne to instruct.
infringe, to breake, to make weake, or feeble.
infuse, to poure in, or steepe in,

§ ingage,

## An Alphabeticall table

§ ingage, lay to pledge, binde himselfe
ingratitude, vnkindnes, or vnthankfulnes
ingenious, wittie, quicke witted
ingine, ⎱ an instrument to do any thing
engine, ⎰ with.
§ ingraue, carue
ingresse,     ⎱ enterance
ingredience, ⎰ in.
ingurgitate, to deuoure vp græedily
inhabite, dwell in
inhabitable, that cannot be dwelt in
inherent, cleauing fast vnto,
inhibit, forbid.
inhibition, forbidding.
inhumane, cruell, vncurteous.
iniunction, commaunding, rule or order.
initiate, to begin, instruct, or enter into
iniurious, wrongfull, or hurtfull,
innauigable, that cannot be sailed vpon
innouate, make newe, young, begin.
innouation, making new, an alteration.
inoculated, grafted, or vnholed.
inordinate, out of order, disordered,
inquinate, to defile, or disgrace
inquisitiue, desirous, and diligent to finde
   out by asking of questions.
inquisition, searching, or inquiring.
                         insatiable,

insatiable, that cannot bee filled or contented.
incend, clime vp, or mount vp
inscription, a title, or note written vppon any place.
inscrutable, that cannot be searched into, or throughly knowne.
insensible, that cannot be felt or perceiued.
inseperable, that cannot be deuided.
insert, to put in, or graft in.
insinuate, cræpe into ones fauour craftilie, also to signifie.
insist, to stay vpon:
insociable, that will not kéepe company.
insolent, proude, disdainefull,
insperge, sprinkle, or cast vpon
inspire, breath or blow into
instable, inconstant, not steddie.
§ install, admit to a place of office, or honour.
instant, earnest, importunate,
instauration, repairing, renewing.
instigation, prouoking, or mouing forward.
instill, to put in, or drop in.
instinct, inward motion, or stirring.
institute, appoint, ordaine, begin, or go in hand with.

F. insult.

## An Alphabeticall table

insulte, to triumphe, or vaunt ouer.
insupportable, not able to be borne
integritie, purenes, innocencie
intelligence, knowledge from others
intemperate, without measure or meane, vnmodest in behauiour
intende, to purpose, or think
intentiue, earnestly bent, and musing
intercession, going betweene, or making intreatie for another,
intercept, preuent, or take before
interchange, exchang
intercourse, mutuall accesse, or passage one to another
interdict, to forbid straitly
§ interest, loane, right, also a part in any thing
interlace, mixe
interline, draw a line betwixt, or to blot out with a penne, and to write betwixt
interlocution, interrupting of anothers speech
intermedle, deale with
intermingle, mixe, or mingle with, or amongst
intermission, foreslowing, a pawsing,
or

of hard English words.

 or breaking of
interpellate, disturbed, hindered
interpreter, expounder
interprete, open, make plaine, to shewe the sence and meaning of a thing
interre, to burie
interrogation, a question, or asking
interrupt, breake of, or let
§ intire, whole, sound, uncorrupt
intestate, that dieth without making a will
intimate, to declare or signifie
intised, drawne, allured
§ intituled, called, noted, written on the beginning
intractable, unrulie, troublesome
intricate, inwrapped, doubtfull, hard to be knowne.
introduction, entrance, or leading in
intrude, to thrust ones selfe into the company of others, or enter in violently
inuade, to set vpon, to lay hold on
inueigle, intice, or deceiue by subtiltie, to intrape.
inueighe, to raile vppon bitterly
§ inuentory, table of goods
inuention, deuise, or imagination
§ inueloped, wrapped in, intangled

     F 2     inuersion,

inuersion, turning vpside downe, turning contrariwise.
§ inuest, to adorne, or decke, or grace.
inueterate, of long continuance, growne in custome:
inuincible, not to be wonne
inuisible, that cannot be seene or perceiued:
inuiolable, that cannot be broken
inuite, bid, request
invndation, an ouerflowing by water,
invocation, a calling vpon any thing with trust in the same
irchin, a hedgehog.
ironie, (g) a mocking speech
irreligious, vngodly, wanting religion
irreprehensible, without reproofe
irreuocable, not to be recalled, or not to bee withdrawne
irritate, to make angry
irruption, breaking in
§ issue, euent, or successe, or end:
iterate, to repeat, or do a thing often, or againe:
iubilee, yeere of ioy, which happened to the Iewes euery fiftie yeere.
iudaisme, worshipping one God without Christ.

iudici-

of hard English words.

iudiciall, belonging to iudgement
iurifdiction, authoritie, to make, or execute lawes in any place.
iuftifie, approue, or make to be accounted good and iuft
iuftified made or accounted for righteous, cleane from sinne.
laborinth, a place so full of windings and turnings, that a man cannot finde the way out of it:
laborious, painfull, full of labour
§ language, a tongue, or speech:
languishing, pining, consuming, wearing away with griefe or sicknes
lapidarie, one skilfull in pretious stones or iewells
§ largesse, or largis: liberalitie
lasciuious, wanton, lecherous
lassitude, wearines
latitude, breadth, largnes
lauacre, a bath or font
lauish, to spend extraordinarily
laud, praise, or commendation
laudable, worthie of praise
laxatiue, loose, purging
§ league, agreement, or couenant of peace.
leake, runne out.

lecherie,

## An Alphabeticall table

lecherie, vnchastnesse, lururie, and vnlawfull lust

§ leete, court

§ legacie, a gift by will, or an ambassage

legate, ambassadour

§ legeiredemaine, lighthandednes, craftie flights, and conueiance

legion, host, or band of souldiers

legitimate, lawfull, according to lawe, and good order

lenitie, gentlenes, mildnes

lethall, mortall, deadly

lethargie, (g) (k) a drowsie and forgetfull disease.

leuell, right, straight

leuitie, lightnes, inconstancie

libertine, loose in religion, one that thinks he may doe what he listeth

libell, a writing, or booke

librarie, a studie, a great number of bookes

licentious, taking libertie to doe euill

ligate, bound, tyed

ligament, the string tying the bones together

§ linage, stocke, kinred

limitation, appointment, how farre any thing shall goe, restraining:

limber,

## of hard English words.

limber, britle
limit, bounds, border, or land marke, also to set such bounds. &c.
liniament, a forme, or proportion by lines, that are drawne
lingell, shoemakers thred
linguist, skilfull in tongues
linquish, to leaue or forsake
lint, cloth
liquide, moist, melted:
literature, learning
litigious, quarrellous, full of strife
§ lieuetenant, deputie in anothers place
litherneffe, flouthfulnes, idlenes
loame, earth, or morter
logicall, (g) belonging to reason
longitude, length
lore, lawe
§ lotarie, casting of lots.
§ lourdin, rude, clownish
§ loyall, obedient, trustie, constant
lumber, old stuffe
lunatick, wanting his wits, at a certaine time of the age of the moone
lumpish, sad or sower countenance.
lustre, glittering, shinning
luxurious, riotous, and ercessiue in pleasure,

An Alphabeticall table
sure, and wontonnesse.

## M

**M**Acerate, to steepe in water, or make cleane
madefie, dip, make wet
maffle, stammer, or stut
magicke, inchaunting, coniuring
magistrate, gouernour
magitian, (g) one vsing witchcraft
magnanimitie, valientnes, courage
magnificence, sumptuousnes
magnifie, to extoll, or praise highly
magnitude, greatnes
§ mayre, leane
maiestie, the stately port and honourable renowne of any
§ maladie, disease
§ malecontent, discontented
malediction, slaundring, ill report, or backbiting, or cursing
malefactor, an euill doer
malepert, saucy, proud, snappish
§ maligne, to hate, with purpose to hurt
§ malignitie, naughtines, malice
malitious, hating, or enuying

manchet,

## of hard English words.

manchet, fine white breade
mandate, a charge, or commaundement
§ maniacque, mad: braine sick
manicle, a fetter, for to bind the hands
manifest, opened, declared or reuealed
manuring, dung, tilling
§ mannage, handle
mansion, an abiding place
manuall, done with the hand
manumisse, to set free, or at libertie
maranatha, (g) accursed
§ marche, goe in aray, or goe forward
margent, edge, or brim of any thing
§ marte, a faire
§ massacre, kill, put to death
martiall, warlike, or valiant, or taking paines and delight in warres
martyre, (g) witnes, one suffering death for the faith of Christ
materiall, of some matter, or importance.
matrixe, wombe
matron, an auncient, sober, and a discreete woman.
mature, ripe, perfect, speedy
§ maugre, despight, against ones will
maxime, a principle, or sure ground in any matter

mechaniall,

mechanicall, ⎫ (g) handie
mechanick, ⎭ craft.
mediatour, aduocate, or suretie, or one making peace betwixt two
medicine, remedie, or cure
mediocritie, a measure, a meane
meditate, muse vpon, bethinke
meditation, the earnest minding or thinking vpon a thing
melancholie, (g) black choler, a humor of solitarines, or sadnes
mellifluous, sweete as hony, yielding much hony.
melody, (g) sweete sounding, or sweete musick
memorable, worthie to be remembred
§ menace, to threaten
menstruous, defiled, or foule.
mentall, belonging to the minde
mercenary, seruing for wages, and hireling.
meridian, pertaining to noone tide
meritorious, that deserueth, or set for aduauntage.
metamorphosis, (g) a changing of one shape, or likenes into another
metaphor, (g) similitude, or the putting ouer

## of hard English words.

ouer of a word from his proper and naturall signification, to a forraine or vnproper signification.

meteors, (g) elementarie bodies, or moyst things, ingendered of vapours in the ayre aboue.

method, (g) an order, or readie way to teach, or doo any thing

methodized, (g) brought into order

metropolitane, (g) of the chiefe citty.

microcosme, (g) a little world

militant, warring, or beeing in warres.

§ miguionise, play the wanton:

ministration, ministring, or seruice, or charge to doo a thing:

minoritie, a mans time vnder age

minutly, smally:

miraculous, meruailous, or wonderfull:

§ mirrour, a looking-glasse

miscreants, infidels, mis-beleeuers:

misprision, concealement of a mans owne knowledge.

misknow, to mistake purposely, to be ignorant of.

mitigate, asswage, qualifie, or pacifie

mixtion, ⎱ mingling, or tempering
mixture, ⎰ together.

        mobilitie,

## An Alphabeticall table

mobilitie, mouing or stirring.
modell, measure,
moderate, temperate, or keeping a meane,
moderation, keeping due order and proportion:
§ moderne, of our time
modest, sober, demure
§ moitie, halfe.
molestation, troubling
mollifie, make soft
momentanie, that which lasteth but a
 while:
moment, weight, or importance, also a
 short time
monarch, (g) one ruling all the kingdoms
 about him
monarchie, (g) the rule of one prince a-
 lone:
monasterie, (g) colledge of monks
monopolie, (g) a licence that none
 shall buy and sell a thing, but one
 alone.
monument, a remembrance of some notable act, as Tombs
moosell, to fetter
§ moote, argue, or dispute a case in law
moralitie, ciuill behauiour.

morall,

### of hard English words.

morall, pertaining to manners, behauior, and life, among men

§ morgage, lay to pawne

morigerous, well mannered

mortall, that endeth ere hauing an end, and dying deadly:

mortifie, kill, or make dead, and sencelesse.

mortuarie, dutie paid for the dead,

motiue, cause moouing, or the thing, and reason, that mooueth to doe any thing.

§ mouldre, make small, turne to dust

mulct, a fine, penaltie, or punishment:

multiplicitie, varietie, or diuersitie of sorts.

mundifie, to make cleane:

munition, defence, supportation, or strength, and plentie of weapons, to resist in warre.

municipall, priuately belonging to a freeman, or burgesse of a cittie.

muses, (g) goddesses of learning.

§ mustaches, the hayre of the vpper lippe.

mutable, changeable, wauering.

mutation,

mutation, change.
muthologie, (g) expounding of the tales of
 the Poets.
mutilate, wanting some part, maimed
mutuall, one for another
myrrhe, (g) sweet gumme
mysterie, (g) a secret, or hid thing:
mysticall, (g) that hath a misterie in it.

# N

Narration, declaration, or report.
 nationall, belonging, or consisting of
 a nation, or kingdome.
natiue, where one was borne, or naturall.
natiuitie, birth, or the day of birth
nauigable, where ships may safely passe, or
 that may be sailed vpon.
nauigation, sayling, or passing by water
necromancie, (g) blacke art, or coniuring,
 by calling vpon spirits.
nectar, a pleasant drinke, which is feyned
 to be the drinke of the gods.
negatiue, that denieth
negotiation, trafficke, or busines
neotericke, (g) one of late time
§ nevewe, a sonne or daughters sonne
 nerue,

## of hard English words.

nerue, sinewe
¶ nete, fine
neutrall, ⎫ of neither
neuter, ⎭ side:
¶ nice, slow, laysie
nicholaitan, (g) an heretike, like Nicholas, who helde that wiues should bee common to all alike.
nominate, to name, or appoint
¶ nonage, a childs time, vnder age
nonresidencie, vnnecessary and wilfull absence, of any one from his place or charge:
¶ nonsuite, not following, or the ending and giuing ouer of a suite
notable, worthy, meete to be regarded and esteemed:
notarie, Scriuener, or register
notifie, to make knowne, or to giue warning of.
notion, inwarde knowledge, or vnderstanding:
notorious, knowne to all, or made plaine and manifest.
noyance, hurt.
noysome, hurtfull,
nullitie, nothing

An Alphabeticall table.

numeration, numbring
nuncupatory, telling, or declaring any thing.
nuptiall, belonging to marriage
nutriment, nourishment

## O

Obdurate, harden, or to make more hard
§ obeisance, obedience
object, laide, or set against, or that whereon any thing resteth, or that where any thing is occupied, or set a worke.
oblation, offering
oblectation, recreation, delight
obliged, bound, or beholden
oblique, crooked, ouerthwart
obliuious, forgetfull
obloquie, euill report
obnoxious, faultie, subiect to danger
obnubilate, to make darke.
obscæne, bawdie, filthy, ribauldrie
obscure, darke, or cloudie
obsequious, seruiceable, readie at hand
obseruant, dutifull, full of diligent seruice.
obsession, besieging, or compassing about
obsolete,

## of hard English words

obsolete, olde, past date, growne out of vse or custome.

obstacle, hinderance or let

obstinate, froward, stubberne, or stiffe in his owne opinion

obstruction, stopping, repressing

obtestate, humble, to beseech, or to call to witnesse:

obtrectation, slaunder, euill report.

obtuse, dull or blunt:

occidentall, belonging to the west

occluding, shutting fast:

§ occurrences, occasions, things that offer themselues by the way:

ocean (g) the maine sea

odious, hatefull, disdainfull

odor, smell, sent, or sauour:

odoriferous, sweet smelling

oeconomicke, (g) things that pertaine to houshold affaires

offensiue, giuing offence, offering wrong, or displeasing

officiall, belonging to an office,

officious, dutifull, dilligent, very readie or willing to please.

oligarchie, (g) a Common-wealth, where two Princes equall haue all the authoritie.

G.

An Alphabeticall table

ritie.
oliuet, place of Oliues:
§ ombrage, shade, harbor, or bower to rest vnder.
ominous, that signifieth some good, or ill lucke:
omit, let passe, ouerslip.
omnipotent, almightie, great, or high
omni-scient, knowing all things
onerous, burdenous, or chargeable
onust, loaden, ouercharged
operation, ⎱ working, or
operatiue, ⎰ effect
opinionate, hauing a good opinion of, or standing on his owne opinion
oportunitie, fitnes to any thing,
oppilation, stopping
oppose, set againe
opposite, contrarie, or set euer against
oppressed, grieued, or violently wronged:
opprobrious, reprochfull, to taunt, reuile, or vpbraide with bad spæches.
oppugne, to labour against, to resist
option, choosing or wishing
oracle, (g) a spæch or aunswere giuen from God:

oratorie,

## of hard English words.

oratorie, eloquent speech:
ordination, ordeyning
ordure, dung, filth,
orifice, mouth
originall, the first, or such as it was at the beginning
organe, (g) an instrument to do any thing with:
ornament, a decking, adorning, or trimming.
orphant, (g) a childe without parents
ossicle, bone:
§ ostages, pledges giuen and taken
ostentation, boasting
orthographie, (g) true writing
§ ouerplus, more then nædeth
§ outragious, fierce, vnreasonable.

## P

Pacifie, to make quiet.
pactation, a couenanting or bargayning.
§ palatine, belonging to a Princes Court, or pallace.
palinodie, (g) a recanting, or vnsaying of any thing

palpable, that may be felt, manifest:
pamphlet, a small treatise, or booke
parable, (g) similitude, or an applying of some thing to our matter, fitly alleaged, for some likenesse which it hath to our purpose.
paradise, (g) place of pleasure
paradoxe, (g) marueilous, or strange speech:
§ paragon, patterne, example
paraleles, (g) lines, or other things as farre off from one another, in one place as in another.
§ paramour, an amorous louer
paraphrase, (g) exposition of any thing by many words.
parasite, (g) a base flatterer, or soothing companion:
parenthesis, (g) a clause contayned in another sentence:
paricide, a murtherer of parents
§ parle, speech, or conference.
parsimonie, thriftines, sparing
participate, partake, deuide, or distribute, to giue, or take part:
particularize, to deuide into parts, and to handle euery particuler.

partition,

of hard English words.

partition, deuision.
passeouer, one of the Iewes feasts, in remembrance of Gods passing ouer them, when he slewe so many of the Egiptians
passion, suffering, griefe
pastorall, belonging to sheapheards
patheticall, (g) vehement, full of passions, or mouing affections
patriarke, (g) chiefe father
patrimonie, fathers, gift, or goods left by a father
§ patronage, defence, protection
patronise, defend
paucitie, fewnes, or smale number
pause, thinke, stay, or rest
§ pauillion, tente
peerelesse, worthie, vnmatchable
peccaui, I haue offended.
peccant, offending, doing amisse
peculiar, proper, or specially belonging
pecuniarie, coyne
pellicles, skinnes
penetrable, that may be pearsed
penitentiarie, one repenting, or doing pennaunce.
penaltie, losse
§ pension, payment, yearely fee

§ pensiue,

## An Alphabeticall table.

§ pensiue, sorrowfull
pentecost, (g) whitsontide
penurie, want or extreame neede
perambulation, a walking about
peregrination, iourneing in a strange land
peremptorie, resolute, short
perforations, holes, or pierced through
perfidious, trayterous, vnfaithfull
perfricated, rubbed much
perilous, dangerous
periclitation, ieopardie, or hazarding
period, (g) the end of a perfect sentence
periurie, forswearing, or breaking of ones oath.
permanent, continuing, or a biding till the end
permission, sufferance, leaue
permit, suffer, giue leaue
permutable, changable
pernitious, dangerous, hurtfull
perpendicular, directly, downe right
perpetrate, to commit, or doe
perpetuitie, continuance for euer
perplexitie, troublesome, griefe, distresse, doubtfulnes
persecute, trouble, afflict, or pursue after.

persist,

## of hard English words.

persist,  ⎫ continew, constantly,
perseuer, ⎭ and resolutely.
personate, to counterfaite, anothers person
perspicacie, quicknes of sight, vnderstanding
perspicuous, euedent, cleare, that may bee seene through
pertinacie, obstinacie, stifnes in opinion
perturbation, disquietnes, or trouble
peruerse, froward, mischeiuous
peruert, ouerthrowe, or turne vp side downe
§ pese, to weigh
peruicacie, obstinacie, stifneckednes
§ pesant, clowne
pester, filled
pest, the plague, or pestilence
pestiferous, contagious, hurtfull
petition, prayer, or request
§ pettigree, stock, or offspring
petulancie, wantonnes, saucines.
phantasie, (g) imagination
philacteries, (g) scroles of parchment, whereon, was writen the tenne commaundements.
physiognomie, (g) knowledge of a mans nature

## An Alphabeticall table

nature by his visage, and countenance
phisicke, (g) medicine, helping, or curing
phlebotomie, (g) letting bloud
phrase, (g) forme of speach
philosophie, (g) study of wisdome
phrensie, (g) madnes
pietie, godlines, holines
§ pillage, spoile in warre, and sacking, of the enemies.
pinguiditie, fatnes, or greasinesse
§ pilot, maister, guider of a ship
§ pionner, digger, or ditcher
piramis, (g) ⎱ a steeple, or other build-
piramides, ⎰ ing, or a pillar broade beneath, and sharpe aboue
pistated, baked
§ pirate, a robber on the sea
§ pittance, short, banquet
placable, easie to be pleased
planet, (g) wandring starre
§ plaintife, the partie complayning
plausible, pleasing, or receiued ioyfully, and willingly
plenitude, fulnes, thicknesse
§ plonge, dippe, or put vnder the water
plume, feather
pluralitie, more then one

pluuiatile,

## of hard English words.

pluuiatile, raine
poeme, (g) verses of a poet
poet, (g) a verse maker
poetesse, a woman poet
pole, (g) the end of the areltree whereon the astronomers, faine the heauens to be turned.
pollicie, a wittie shift
poligamie, (g) hauing moe wiues then one
polish, to deck, or make faire, smooth, sleeke, or shining
pollute, defile, or distaine, or make filthie
pomegarnet, or pomegranet, (k) fruite
pompe, the countenance of things in furniture, and setting forth to the outward shewe.
ponderous, weightie, heauie
pontificall, lordly, sumptuous, bishoplike.
portable, that may be carried with ease.
popular, seeking the fauour of the people by all meanes possible:
populus, full of people:
popularitie, pleasing the people,
position, a question to be disputed of
posteritie,

## An Alphabeticall table

posteritie, they that come after by birth, the age after vs.

postscript, written after

potion, a drinke,

§ pourtrait, draw the forme, or proportion of a thing

practicall, (g) ⎫
practique, ⎬ practising.
pragmaticall, ⎭

§ preamble, forespæch, a flourish, entrance, or assay.

precedent, going before

precept, a rule giuen, an admonition, or commaundement.

precinct, compasse appointed:

predecessor, one that was in place before another.

predestinate, to appoint before.

prediction, afore telling, or prophecying

predominante, ruling

preheminence, excellent, rule, authoritie ouer others

preface, a speech before the matter it selfe

prefigurate, forshewe by a figure

prefixed, set in the fore part

pregnant, wittie, substantiall, with child

## of hard English words.

child,
preiudicate, giuing his iudgment, before he knoweth the man, or matter
preiudice, hindering ones cause, sentence, an opinion deliuered before knowledge of any thing
preludium, an entrance to any thing
premeditation, thinking of a matter before hand
§ premunire, forfeiture of goods
preoccupation, a preuenting by speech or other wayes
preordination, appointing before
preparatiue, that which maketh fit or prepareth
preposterous, disorder, froward, topsiteruie, setting the cart before the horse, as we vse to say
prerogatiue, priuiledge, or authoritie before another
presage, to tell before, to betoken, to foresee.
presbitarie, (g) eldership
prescience, foreknowledge
prescript, decree, or assignement
prescription, limitation, or appointing a certaine compasse.

preseruatiue,

preseruatiue, that which defendeth
president, a chiefe, ruler next vnder the highest
prest, reacte
presuppose, faine a thing to be before it is.
pretermit, to passe ouer, to forget willinglie.
preterlapsed, passed, or gone past
pretext, an excuse, colour, or pretence
preuarication, collusion, or betraying of a cause or matter, for want of more earnest speech.
primitiue, ⎫ first, or formost,
primarie, ⎭ or excellent,
prioritie, being in the formost place, or in greater excellencie and superioritie then another.
pristine, old, wonted, or accustomed
priuation, depriuing, vtter taking away, or withdrawing
priuiledge, prerogatiue, or liberty, more then others haue
probable, that may be easilie proued to be true.
probation, alouance, tryall
probleme (g) proposition, or sentence

in

## of hard English words.

in manner of a question.
proceede, goe forth, or goe forward,
processe, proceeding, passing forward,
procliuitie, inclination to any thing
proctcur, a factour, or solicitor.
procrastinate, to defer, or delay
prodigall, too riotous in spending
prodigious, wonderfull, giuing an ill
    signe.
prodition, betraying, treason
profane, vngodly, not consecrated, or vn-
    hallowing that which was holy.
profound, deepe, or high.
profunditie, deepenes.
profusion, pouring out wastfully,
progenie, offspring, generation, or issue of
    children.
progenitor, a fore-father, or grandfather.
prognosticate, (g) to know or giue out be-
    fore-hand, or to tell afore-hand what
    shall happen.
progresse, a going forward:
prohibit, to forbid, or giue straight charge
    to the contrary.
proiect, a plot, or wise contriuing of any
    thing, or casting forth
prolixe, tedious, long, or large.
                       prolo=

## An Alphabeticall table

prolocutor, a speaker for another
prologue, a preface, or forespæch
prolong, stretch out, or defer.
promerit, desert:
promote, to honor or aduaunce to greater dignitie, and higher place
prompt, ready, quicke:
promulgation, publishing openly, or proclaiming.
prone, ready, or inclining
§ prowesse, valiantnesse
propagate, to enlarge, or multiply.
prophecie, (g) foretell, or expound
prophet, (g) he that prophecieth
propitiation, a sacrifice to appease Gods displeasure:
propitiatorie, that which reconcileth, or which purchaseth mercie, at the mercie seate:
propitious, not displeased, fauourable
proportion, equalnes, measure:
propose, propound, set before, or shew
proprietie, propertie, owing, or challenging as his owne, and none others:
proroge, put off, prolong, deferre
proscription, a condemnation, or banishnishment proclaimed, or an open sale.

## of hard English words.

sale.
prose, that writing which is not verse.
proselite, (g) stranger converted to our religion or manners:
prosequute, follow after, or finish
prospect, a sight a farre off.
prostitute, set open for vncleanesse, to set forth to sale.
prostrate, to cast downe, or fall downe flat on the ground.
protect, defend, saue, or couer:
protest, to affirme, and declare openly:
protract, deferre, or prolong, or draw out at length:
prouident, foreseeing with wise consideration, and prouiding aforehand
prouinciall, iurisdiction, belonging to a prouince, or outcountry
prouocation, prouoking, enforcing, vrging pressing, or alluring
prudence, wisdome, wittinesse
publicane, a farmer, or common man of a Cittie:
§ pulers, dust, or powders
puluirisated, beaten, or broken into dust, or powder.
purifie, purge, scoure, or make cleane

§ pursuite,

## An Alphabeticall table

§ pursuit, following after
putrifie, to waxe rotten, or corrupted as a sore.
pusillanimitie, faint-hartednes, cowardlinesse.
§ puissant, strong, valiant

## Q

Quadrangle, foure-cornered  
quadrant, } foure square, or  
quadrate, } a quarter.  
quartane, belonging to, or comming euery fourth day.
queach, thicke heape
querimonious, full of complaining, and lamentation:
§ quintessence, chiefe vertue, drawne by art out of many compounds together.
quondam, hæretofore, in times past
§ quote, cite, preuent
quotidian, daily, that happeneth euery day.

## R

Racha, fie, a note of extreame anger, signified by the gesture of the person that speaketh it, to him ẏ he speaketh to.

radicall,

## of hard English words.

radicall, partaining to the roote, naturall:
radiant, shining bright:
§ rallie, gather together men dispersed, and out of order.
§ rampar, fortification, or trench
rapacitie, ⎱ violent, catching, extortion, or
rapine, ⎰ pillage, or rauening.
raritie, scarsenes, fewnes
ratifie, establish, or confirme
§ rauish, take away by force,
§ raunged, ordered, or put into order
reachlesse, carelesse, or negligent:
reall, substantiall, or that is indeede subsisting:
recantation, an vnsaying of that which was said before
recapitulation, a briefe rehearsing againe of any thing
receptacle, a place to receiue things in
reciprock, or ⎱ that hath respect back a-
reciprocall, ⎰ gaine to the same thing.
recite, rehearse, or repeate
reclaime, to gainesay, or call back againe:
§ recognissance, acknowledging, or a signe of acknowledging, and confessing any thing.
§ recoile, goe backe.

H.                              recon=

## An Alphabeticall table

reconcile, bring into fauour, or to make peace betwixt.

records, writings layde vp for remembrance:

recreate, refresh, comfort,

recourse, a running backe againe

rectifie, to make right or straight

redeeme, purchase, buy againe, or raunsome.

redemption, a buying againe

§ redresse, correct, amend.

reduce, to bring back againe

reduction, a bringing backe

redundant, ouerflowing, or abounding too much.

reduplicated, doubled.

reedifie, build vp againe

reestablish, to settle againe as before

refection, a refreshing, or recreating.

refell, to confute, or proue false

reference, a pointing at, or alluding to

referre, put ouer, or to report himselfe vnto.

refine, repaire, renue, or amend

reflection, casting backe, or bowing, turning backe againe

refractarie, wilful in opinion, obstinate.

§ refraine,

of hard English words.

¶ refraine, abstaine from, kéepe in
refuge, succour, or place of safetie
refulgent, shining bright
refute, to disproue
regall, princly, like a King
regenerate, borne againe
regeneration, a new birth,
regent, a Gouernor, or Ruler
regiment, gouernment, guidance, rule, or dominion.
register, kalender, a reckoning booke
regrator, huckster, or one that buyeth any thing, and trims it vp to make it more salable.
regresse, returning backe againe
reguler, made according to rule and order.
reiect, fling, cast away, or refuse
¶ reioynder, a thing added afterwards, or is when the defendant maketh answere to the replication of the plaintife.
reiterate, to doo, or repeate againe the same thing often.
relapse, back-sliding.
relate, report, rehearse, or declare
relation, pointing, reporting, or referring
relatiue, hauing relation vnto
relaxation, refreshing, releasing,

P 2.                release,

## An Alphabeticall table

release, frée, quit:
§ reliefe, ayde, helpe, or succour.
reliques, the remainder.
relinquish, to leaue, or forsake
relish, tast:
remarkable, able or worthy to be marked againe:
remisse, loose, negligent, or dull, or too fauourable.
remit, forgiue, release, or acquite.
§ remorse, prick of conscience
remote, set a farre of
remuneration, rewarding, or requiting
renouate, renew, or repaire
renounce, forsake, or resigne
§ renoume, credite, fame, report
reparation, a renewing
§ repast, foode
§ repeale, call backe againe
repell, to put, or thrust backe
repercussiue, striking, or rebounding back againe.
replenish, fill:
replete, filled full
repleueying, redéeming of a gage, or any thing in prison:
replie, to confirme a spéech before vttered.
§ repose,

## of hard English words.

§ repose, put, wholly to rest
represent, expresse, beare shew of a thing
represse, put downe, to let or stop
reprobate, a cast away, out of fauour, a forlorne person, and one past grace
§ reproch, shame, disgrace
republicke, a Common-wealth
repugnancie, contrarietie, or disagreement
repugnant, contrarie
repugne, to resist, oppose, stand against
repulse, to put, or driue backe
repute, account, or esteeme:
requisite, required as necessary:
reserue, to keepe for the time to come
resident, abiding or cōtinuing in his place.
resignation, a yeelding vp, or restoring of anie thing.
resigne, giue ouer to another
resist, withstand
resolue, to vnloose, to satisfie, to purpose constantly,
§ resort, accesse, or comming to
respiration, breathing out.
§ respite, defer, or delay the time, to breath in:
resplendent, shining bright
responses, answers.

restaura=

## An Alphabeticall table

restauration, restoring, or reuiuing
restitution, restoring, satiffaction
restrained, bæing held in, or bridelded
resume, take againe
§ retire, to giue backe, or goe back
reteyne, kæpe backe
retort, to turne, or wrest backward
§ retract, going backe
retrograde, going backward
§ reuell, play the wanton
reuerend, worthy of reuerence
reueale, lay open, disclose, or make known a matter of secret
reuert, to returne
§ reuenewe, rents comming in
reuoke, to call backe, or draw back
§ reuolt, forsake one, to goe to another his enemie:
reuolue, to tosse vp and downe, to determine well of in the mind
rhetorician, (g) learned and skilfull in rhetoricke.
rhetoricke, (g) art of eloquence
rheume, (g) or catarre, a distilling of humors from the head
ridiculous, that deserueth to be laughed at in scorne.

rifle,

## of hard English words.

§ rifle, search, take away by violence
rigorous, cruell, and hard
§ rinse, wash, make cleane by washing
§ riuall, one suing, and striuing for the same thing.
rubrick, a lawe, or title
§ royalty, gouernement, rule, authority
rudiment, first instruction, or principle
rubicunde, red, or ruddie
ruinous, ready to fall
ruminate, to chewe ouer againe, to studie earnestlie vppon
runnagate, one that runneth away, and wandreth abroad.
rupture, breach, or bursting
rurall,      ⎱ clownish, vplandish, or chur-
rusticall,   ⎰ lish, and vnmannerly
saboth, rest
sacrament, holie signe, oath, or misterie
sacred, holy, consecrated
sacrifice, an offering
sacrificule, a little offering
sacriledge, church robbing, the stealing of holy things
§ safeconduit, safe keeping or safe guiding
sagacitie, sharpnes of wit, witnes
saint, holy one

§ sallie,

## An Alphabeticall table

§ sallie, to step out from the rest of the armie, to make a skermish
saluation, a sauing
salubritie, wholesomnes
sanctifie, hallowe, make holy, or keepe holy
sanctification, holines
sanctitie, } holi-
sanctmonie, } nes.
sanctuarie, holy place, saue, defend
sandals, (g) slippers
sanguine, bloudy, or of the colour of bloud.
sanitie, health, or soundnes
sapience, wisdome
satiate, filled, satisfied
satietie, fulnes, plentie
satisfaction, a making amends for wrongs, or displeasures
satisfactorie, that dischargeth, or answereth for
saturate, filled, or glutted
saturitie, fulnesse, or plentifulnesse
§ sauage, wild, cruell, or rude
satyre, (g) a nipping and scoffing verse
satericke, } belonging to a
satiricall, } scoffing verse.

scandalize,

## of hard English words

scandalize, (g) to offend, or giue occasion, to mislike
scandall, (g) an offence, or stumbling block
§ scarifie, to launce, or open a sore
§ scedule, obligation, or bill of ones hand.
schisme, breach, or diuision in matters of religion
schismatike, that maketh a schisme
science, knowledge, or skill
scripture, writing
scruple, doubt, difficultie
scrutiny, diligent search, inquiry
scrupulous, full of doubts
scurrilitie, saucie, scoffing
seclude, shutout, or put a part
sectarie, one whom many other doe followe in opinion.
sect, a diuersitie in opinion from others
section, a deuision, or parting
secular, worldly, of the world
secundarie, the second, or of the second sort
securitie, carelessenes, feare of nothing
sediment, that which sinketh to the bottome.
seditious, making contention
seduce, deceiue, or deuide, or leade aside

sedulitie,

## An Alphabeticall table

sedulitie, dilligence or carefulnes
§ segniorie, lordship
segregate, to set a part, or seperate
§ seize, to forfaite to the prince
select, to choose out from others
semicircle, halfe a circle, or compasse
seminarie, a nurserie, or seede plot for young trees, or grafts
senator, alderman, or counsailer
sense, feeling, or perceiuing
sensible, easily felt, or perceiued
sensuall, brutish, pertaining to the flesh, and bodily sence
sententious, full of fine sentences, and speeches.
§ sentinell, watching by night
seperation, deuiding, seuering, or parting one from another
sepulcher, graue, or tombe
sepulte, burie, or lay in the ground
sequele, following, or that which followeth.
sequester, to put into an indifferent mans hands, to deuide, keepe or iudge of
serious, earnest, or of waight, and importance
serpentine, of, or like a serpent

seruile,

## of hard English words.

seruile, slauish
seruitude, bondage, or slauery
seuere, sharpe, curst, or cruell
seueritie, sharpnes, roughnes
sex, kind
shackle, fetter
significant, plainely signifying
similie, or ⎱ likenes, or re-
similitude, ⎰ semblance.
§ simonie, when spirituall matters, are bought, and solde for money
simplicitie, plainenes
sinister, vnhappie, bad, vnlawefull, or contrarie.
sincere, pure, vncorrupt, vnmingled, or without dissimulation
singularitie, being like no body else, in opinion, or other wayes
situation, setting, or standing of any place.
sleight, guile, craft, or subtiltie.
smatterer, some what learned, or one hauing but a little skill
snatch, to take hastely
snipperings, pairings
§ soare, mount high
sociall, or ⎱ fellowe like, one that wil
sociable, ⎰ keepe company, or one with
whom

## An Alphabeticall table

whom a man may easily keepe company.

societie, fellowship, company
sodomitrie, when one man lyeth filthylie with another man
§ soiourne, remaine in a place
solace, comfort
solemnize, to doe a thing with great pompe, reuerence, or deuotion
§ solicite, moue
solide, sound, heauie, not hollowe
solitarie, alone, or without company
solution, vnloosing, or paying
sophister, (g) cauiller, or craftie disputer
sophistikation, ⎫ a cauilling, deceit-
sophisme,         ⎭ full speech.
§ sotte, foole, dunse
§ soueraigne, chiefe, or highest in authoritie.
§ source, waue, or issuing foorth of water
§ soile, foule, or durtie
spatious, large, wide, or broade
specifie, signifie, or declare particularly
specke, spot, or marke
spectacle, a thing to be looked at
sperme, seede
sphære, (g) round circle, or any thing that
is

## of hard English words.

is round
spicerie, a place to keepe spice in
splendent, glittering, shinning
splene, milt
spongeous, like a sponge
spousals, betrothings, or contracts
spume, fome, or froth
stabilitie, surenes, certaine, strong
stable, sure, stedfast
stablished, sure, confirmed, one made strong
station, a standing place
statue, an image of wood, or any other matter
stature, height, bignes
sterilitie, barrennes
stigmaticall (g) knauish, noted for a lewd naughty fellowe, burnt through the eare for a rogue.
stile, manner, or forme of speech, or writing
stillatorie, a distilling place
stipendarie, one that serueth for wages
stipulation, a solemne couenant
strangle, kill, or hang
stratageme, a pollicie, or wittie shift in warre

stricke,

An Alphabeticall table.

strict, straight, seuere, or sharpe.
strictnes, narrownes, or smalenes
studius, diligent, desirous of learning.
stupefie, to astonish
stupiditie, astonishment, dulnes
suasorie, containing counsaile and exhortation
subalterne, succeeding, following by course and order.
subdued, kept vnder, or brought in subiection
sublimity, height, highnes
sublime, set on high, lift vp
submisse, lowly, humble, brought in subiection
§ suborne, to procure false witnes
subscribe, write vnder, or to agree with another in any matter
subsequent, following hard by
subsiste, to abide, or haue a being
substitute, a deputie, or one set in place of another.
substract, ⎱ take from, with-
subtract, ⎰ drawe.
subtill, craftie, wilie, deceitfull
subuerte, to turne vpside downe, to destroy.

## of hard English words.

stroy.
succeede, followe, or come in anothers place
successor, he that comes in place of another
succincte, shorten, or briefe, or close girt vp
suggest, prompt, tell priuily, or put in mind of.
suffixed, fastened vnto
suffocate, to choake vp, or strangle
suffragane, a bishops deputie, or helper
suffrage, consent, or voice, or helpe
suggest, a high place, or pulpit
sulphure, brimstone
§ summarie, an abridgement, or thing drawne into a lesse compasse
summarilie, briefely, in fewe words
§ sumptuous, costly, rich
supererogation, giuing more then is required.
superabundant,  ⎫ needelesse, vnnecessarie
                ⎬ ouer much, that which
superfluous,    ⎭ runneth ouer.
superficies, vpper side, or out side
superficiall, taking onely the outside, and vttermost part

superio=

## An Alphabeticall table

superioritie, place aboue another

superscription, writing aboue

superstitious, fearefull in matters of religion without cause, one giuen to false and vaine religion

supplant, ouerthrowe, or trippe, with the feete.

supplement, that which maketh vp, or addeth that which wanteth in any thing

§ supple, make soft, or gentle

supplication, request, or prayer

§ suppliant, humbly intreating

support, beare vp, or conuaie vnder

supposition, supposing, thinking, iudging, or imagining.

suppresse, keepe downe, conceale, or keepe secret

supreme, the highest, or greatest

supremacie, chiefedome, or highest place in authoritie aboue all others

§ surcease, to giue ouer, or cease

§ surcharge, ouercharge, hurt

§ surmount, ⎱ exceede, or
surpasse, ⎰ goe beyond

surplus, more then inough

§ surprise, to come vpon, and vnawares, and to take of a suddaine.

§ surrender,

of hard English words.

surrender, to yield up to another
§ surrogate, a deputie in anothers place
§ suruiue, ouer liue, or liue after
suspense, doubt, or vncertaintie
sustained, suffered, or endured
swaine, clowne
swarth, darke, or blackish
swarue, goe away erre.
sycophant, (g) tale bearer or false accu-
    ser.
symball, (g) creede
symmetrie, (g) a due proportion of one part
    with another
sympathie, (g) fellowelike feeling.
symptome, (g) any griefe, or passion, fol-
    lowing a disease
synagogue, (g) place of assemblie
synode, (g) a generall assemblie, or mee-
    ting

## T

§ Tablet, little table
tabernacle, a tent, or pauilion
tacite, still, silent, saying nothing
taciturnitie, silence, or keeping counsaile
§ tapish, lie downe, hide it selfe
                F.                    taxed,

An Alphabeticall table

taxed, seised, appointed to pay a subsidie
temerarious, rash, vnaduised, or haire-
   braine
temeritie, rashnes, vnaduisednes
temperance, sobrietie, moderation
temperate, keeping a meane, moderate
temperature,  ⎱ temperatenes, meane,
temperament, ⎰ or due proportion.
tempestuous, boisterous, or stormie
temporall, that which indureth but for a
   certaine time
temporarie, for a time
temporise, to serue the time, or to followe
   the fashions, and behauiour of the
   time.
tenacitie, nigardnes
tenuitie, smalenesse, or slendernesse
§ tenure, hold, or manner of holding a possession
termination, ending, finishing, or boun-
   ding
§ teritorie, region, or the countrie lying a-
   bout the citie.
tertian, belonging to euery third day
terrestriall, earthly
testament, last will
testification, witnessing

testimonies,

### of hard English words

testimonies, records, depositions or witnessings.

tetrarch, (g) gouernour, or prince of a fourth part, of a country

theologie, (g) diuinitie, the science of liuing blessedly for euer

theoricke, (g) the contemplation, or inward knowledge, of any art

throne, (g) a kings seate, or chaire of estate.

throtle, strangle, hang, or torment

thwart, crosse, or mock

thwite, shaue

timerous, fearefull, abashed

timiditie, fearefulnes

tincture, a colour, die, or staining

tolerable, that which may be suffered

tone, (g) a tune, note, or accent

§ trace, find out by the foote steppes

tractable, easie to handle, or easie to be entreated

tractate, a treatise, or booke, handling any matter

§ tracte, a space, or length

tradition, a deliuering from one to another.

traduce, to slaunder, reproach, or defame,

to

## An Alphabeticall table
to bring in, or drawe from one to another.

§ traffique, bargayning
tragedian, a maker, or player, of a tragedy.
tragedie, (g) a solemne play, describing cruell murders and sorrowes
tragicall, cruell, sorrowfull, like a tragedy.
§ traine, followers, company
tranquilitie, quietnes, or calmenes, or rest
transcendent, climing ouer, mounting vp
transferre, conceiue ouer
transforme, } change from one fashion, to
transfigure, } another
transgresse, breake, offende or goe ouer
§ transitorie, soone passing away, not long lasting.
translation, altering, chaunging
transmigration, a passing from one place, to dwell in another.
transmutation, a change from one place, to another
transome, lintell ouer a dore
transparent, that which may bee seene through
transport, carie ouer, from one place to another.

transpose,

## of hard English words.

transpose, change
transubstantiation, a changing of one substance into another
§ trauerse, strike, or thrust through
triangle,   ⎱ three cor-
triangular, ⎰ nered.
tribe, a company, ward, or hundred
§ tribulation, trouble, sorrowe, anguish
tribunall, iudgement seate
§ tributarie, that payeth tribute
§ tribute, rent, pension, or subsidie
tripartite, threefold, or deuided into three parts.
triuiall, common, of smale estimation
triumph, great ioy outwardly shewed
triumphant, reioycing for the conquest
§ trompe, deceiue
troncheon, stake, or billet
trophee, a victorie, or any thing set in signe of victorie
tropickes, (g) circles in the heauen which when the sunne comes too, beginnes to returne againe.
§ troupe, company, or band of men in an army
truce, peace
trucheman, an interpreter

F 3 truculent,

## An Alphabeticall table

truculent, cruell, or terrible in countenance.

crunchion, weapon.

tumult, vprore, hurly-burly or insurrection

tumultuous, ⎫ troublous, disturbing
turbulent, ⎭ or disquieting.

tiranize, vse crueltie

type, (g) figure, example, shadowe of any thing.

## V

Vacant, voyde, or emptie

vacation, a time of ceasing from labour

§ vagabonde, runnagate, one that will stay no where

validitie, strength, or force, or value

valour, force, courage, or strength

value, price, or estimation

§ vanquish, ouercome, preuaile, conquer, or ouerthrowe

vapor, moisture, ayre, hote breath, or reaking

varietie, change, or diuersitie

§ vassall, slaue, client

vaste, spoiled, destroyed, emptie

§ vauntcourers,

## of hard English words.

§ vauntcourers, forerunners
vbiquitie, presence of a person in all places.
varnish, shine
vegetable, springing, or growing, as herbes.
vehement, earnest, strong, forcible
vendible, saileable, easie, and readie to be solde
venerable, worshipfull, or reuerende
veneriall, ⎱ fleshly, or lecherous,
venerous, ⎰ giuen to lecherie.
veniall, that which may be pardoned
vente, saleable
ventricle, the stomacke which receiues the meate
venuste, faire, beautifull
verbatim, word by word, perfectly
verbositie, much talking, and pratling
veritie, truth
verifie, to proue it to be true
versifie, make verses
vertigiousnes, lightnes, or a swimming of the heade
vestall, a nunne, vowing chastitie
vesture, ⎱ garment, attire, or
vestiment, ⎰ clothing.
§ viand, victailes

§ viceroy,

## An Alphabeticall table

§ viceroy, one set as a deputie in the Kings place.

virinitie, neighbourhoode

vicegerent, one that supplyeth the place of another.

vicious, faultie, or full of vice

victorious, that hath gotten many victories.

viewe, behold, marke, or consider, or looke vppon

vigilance, watchfull, dilligence.

vigour, strength, courage, or force

vincible, that may be wonne, or easily ouercome.

vineyard, orchard of grapes

violate, to transgresse, defile, deflowre, or breake.

violent, forcible, cruell, iniurious:

viperine, like a viper, or of a viper.

virago, a woman of a manly courage

virulent, full of poyson, venemous.

§ visage, face, forme, or shape.

vision, sight, apparition, or a phantasie.

visible, that may be seene

visitation, going to see

vitall, liuely, or pertayning to life.

vitiate, to corrupt, or deflower, and defile.

viuificent,

## of hard English words.

viuificent, liuely, or full of strength
viuifie, to quicken, or make aliue:
vlcer, bile, or botch
vlcerate, to blister, or make full of sores
vmpire, iudge:
vnconceaueable, not able to be conceiued
vnaccessible, that cannot be come to.
vnanimitie, one consent of hart and mind
vnction, annointing
vndecent, vncomlie
vndermine, graue, dig
vnguent, an oyntment, or fat iuyce
vnitie, } peace, or
vnion, } concord
vnitie, to make one thing of two, or moe, to couple, or ioyne:
vnsatiable, not content
vniformitie, one and the same fashion
vniuersall, generall, common:
vocall, with the voice, or pertaining to the voyce:
vocation, calling, estate, or trade of life.
vnsatiable, that neuer hath enough, neither can be satisfied:
volubilitie, swiftnes, or inconstancie
voluntary, of the owne accord, without being taught, or vrged.

voluptuous,

# An Alphabeticall table

voluptuous, giuen to pleasure

§ vpbraid, rise in ones stomack, cast in ones teeth:

vrbanitie, curtesie, good manners, or gentlenes:

vrgent, earnestly calling vpon, forcing

§ vsurpe, take vnlawfull authoritie, or to vse against right and reason.

§ vtensiles, things necessary for our vse in house-keeping, or in a trade.

vtilitie, profit

vlgar, common, much vsed

## Z

ZOdiack, (g) a circle in the heauen, wherein be placed the 12. signes, and in which the Sunne is moued.

FINIS.